THE ANNALS

AND

PARISH REGISTER

OF

95 - 1050

ST. THOMAS AND ST. DENIS PARISH,

IN

SOUTH CAROLINA,

FROM 1680 TO 1884.

COLLECTED AND ARRANGED

BY

ROBERT F. CLUTE, RECTOR.

CLEARFIELD COMPANY
REPRINTS & REMAINDERS

Originally Published
Charleston, South Carolina
1884

Reprinted
Genealogical Publishing Co., Inc.
Baltimore, 1974

Reprinted for Clearfield Company Inc. by
Genealogical Publishing Co. Inc.
Baltimore, MD 1989

Library of Congress Cataloging in Publication Data
St. Thomas and St. Denis Parish, South Carolina.
  The annals and parish register of St. Thomas and St. Denis Parish, in South Carolina, from 1680 to 1884.

  Reprint of the 1884 ed. printed by Walker, Evans & Cogswell, Charleston, S. C.
  1. Registers of births, etc.—St. Thomas and St. Denis Parish, S. C. 2. St. Thomas and St. Denis Parish, S. C.—Genealogy. I. Clute, Robert F., comp. II. Title.
F277.S24S24 1974   929'.3757'91   73-17368
ISBN 0-8063-0601-7

1884.

PARISH OF ST. THOMAS AND ST. DENIS,

DIOCESE OF SOUTH CAROLINA.

Rector.

REV. ROBERT F. CLUTE, D. D.

WARDENS AND VESTRYMEN FOR THE YEAR.

Wardens.

J. COMING BALL.   WM. L. VENNING.

Vestrymen.

G. E. MANIGAULT, M. D.

JOHN SHOOLBRED,	WM. L. VENNING, JR.
SAMUEL SANDERS,	ROBERT N. CLUTE.
WM. M. S. LESESNE.	CH'S F. HANCKEL, JR.

Secretary and Treasurer.

CH'S F. HANCKEL, JR.

Finance Committee.

G. E. MANIGAULT, M. D.   WM. L. VENNING.
SAMUEL SANDERS.

Solicitors.

RUTLEDGE & YOUNG, Charleston.

INTRODUCTORY NOTES.

1. Two hundred years are not a very long time, and yet owing to the neglect of recording details, much interesting and valuable parochial history has been lost, and the generations of families broken and confused. Had the Rectors or Registrars given a thought to the probable wishes of posterity, our records would doubtless be full and minute. Christ Church has the most complete of any I have read; the proceedings of the vestry extending back to about the beginning of the last century. Some of the incidents are sorrowfully amusing. St. Michael's, of Charleston, and St. Mark's Clarendon, have lost their records by fire; St. John's Berkley, by military theft; Beaufort, by decay; St. Thomas, some by fire and others misplaced. It is to be desired that the vestries of those parishes who retain any record of their past will follow this example of their brethren of St. Thomas and St. Denis, and print them for the benefit of the Church and State. The present depositories of these archives are by no means fireproof, and the publication of these annals and registers, placed in public or private libraries, seems to be the only mode of preserving the few remains of our parochial history.

2. To save expense it has been found expedient to give the historical facts without comment, and hence the form of annals.

The chairman of the vestry, during a recent visit at the North, sought information at the libraries of Harvard and Yale, for the most comprehensive method of arranging the registers, but found nothing satisfactory. The plan adopted seems to be the most simple. Where the same name is in each list it can be easily traced. The names of the wives are given alphabetically among those of their husbands. In the baptismal register the date of birth is also given; the families of the same name grouped according to date. In the burial list the date of death is generally given; that of burial only when the former is not given; sometimes both. It seems as if the registrars had noted acts performed by the rectors in other parishes, and also of deaths of parishioners elsewhere. For nearly four years I have been reading and examining every source of information of which I could learn. There was a vast amount of notes, but when digested the remains are the meagre annals presented. The present arrangement of the old records of the parish was the most troublesome, and four written reviews were required before no error could be found.

I am much indebted to the kind aid of Langdon Cheves, Esq., and especially in the preparation of the history of the Beresford Family, which it is proposed to publish hereafter in the pamphlet concerning the Beresford Bounty Fund. Many additions have been made to the burial list from inscriptions in the several cemeteries, of which no record had been made from 1790 to 1823. By this neglect we have lost the list of marriages and births or baptisms during the same time. It is evident, from a study of the registers, that some dates are erroneous; the same name spelled differently; that very many of the French records are wanting; that there was great neglect to obtain full returns from many families, and in some cases of entire generations.

New matter may hereafter come to light. I have done the best I could with my material amid professional duties and much family sickness.

The apparently rapid extinction of the parish, ecclesiastically; the former neglect to preserve records; the use it may be for diocesan church history, family genealogies, &c., have influenced the Vestry to perform this, which they believe to be, a religious and patriotic duty.

3. The Dutarque is the only one of the original families remaining in the parish. Now Dutart.

4. The three cemeteries are known by the names of

(1) The Brick Church—the Parish Church.

(2) The Old Ruins—Charity Meeting—Methodist Church.

(3) Pompion Hill—The Chapel.

5. It is my impression, though I have forgotten to search the Journals of the Diocese in charge of the Registrar, that, like many of the Colonial Churches, the Parish Church and Pompion Hill Chapel have never been consecrated, unless by the devout worship of successive generations.

6. B. B. S. among burials—Beresford Bounty Scholars.

7. There are a few entries of free negroes in the first register, or until 1790. In the second, are the names, baptisms, confirmations, communions, marriages, burials, &c., of very many slaves until the close of the late war. The names of owners are also recorded.

The Rev. Francis H. Rutledge was the first Rector to record confirmations, communicants, &c. The last register contains the arrangement of the former two, as herein printed, with the inscriptions copied from the tomb-stones, lists of parishioners, families, communicants, confirmations, &c., from 1827, and other information thought worthy of preservation.

8. St. Thomas and the other parishes were originally created Church of England, and not civil parishes, and so continued until South Carolina became a State. Ramsay Eccles. Hist., p. 5.

9. The authorities consulted in the preparation of this work are :

The Parish Registers of St. Thomas and St. Denis, of Christ Church and St. Philip's, Charleston.

The Cemetery Inscriptions of St. Thomas and St. Denis.

The Journals of the Diocese.

Colonial and State Statutes.

Colonial Chancery Reports.

Wills in Probate Office.

Hist'l Cols. of the Hist'l Soc., South Carolina.

Irving's Days on the Cooper River.

Memorial Services in St. Philip's.

Dalcho's Hist. of the Church in So. Ca.
Humphrey's Hist. Soc. Prop. Gos. For. Parts, ed. 1730.
Shipp's Hist. Methodism in So. Ca.
Howatt's Hist. of the Province of So. Ca.
Rivers' Sketch of the Proprietary Government.
Gibbes' Documentary Hist. of So. Ca.
Ramsay's Hist. of So. Ca.

R. F. C.

BERESFORD HALL, ST. THOMAS PARISH, June 1, 1884.

THE ANNALS

OF

ST. THOMAS AND ST. DENIS PARISH,

SOUTH CAROLINA.

The peninsula formed by the Cooper and Wando Rivers, was probably settled by a few families, before Old Charlestown was removed to Oyster Point. Gradually others found homes on the banks of both streams, until about 1680 they had extended to the limit of navigation. These were chiefly from England. During the next five years, thirty-two French families Shipp Hist., p. 34, settled in the interior, mostly from French Quarter 35. Creek to the Cooper. The greater number had been sent to the Province by King Charles II., at his own expense, in two vessels, at the earlier date. They cultivated the vine, olive and mulberry, and engaged in the manufacture of wine, oil and silk. A small church was erected, in which divine worship was occasionally celebrated by the Rev. Mr. Prioleau and the Rev. Dr. LeJeau. The services were well attended. The names of these Huguenot families, as the earliest Par. Reg. on record in the Parish Register, are supposed to have been Bonneau, Bochett, Bellin, Bremar, Brabant, Bossard, Carriere, DuPre, Dutarque, DeLonguemar, Durant, Duberdeaux, Dubois, Guerin, Joly, Jaudon, LeJeau, Leroux, Lesesne, Mouzon, Marbeuf, Poitvine, Roulain, St. Martin, Simons or Symonds, Syer, Sallens, Tresvin, Verine, Verone, Videau and Warbeuf. If there is any public record extant of the original grants of their lands, a more correct list might be made.

1702.

The Society for the Propagation for the Gospel in Foreign parts, chartered June 16, 1700, by William III., sent out the Rev. Samuel Thomas, as a Missionary to the Yemassee Indians; but on his arrival he

Humphrey, page 81.

was appointed by Governor Sir Nathaniel Johnson to succeed the Rev. Mr. Corbin in ministering to the families settled on the three branches of the Cooper River, and to make Goose Creek his chief place of residence. He reported that the French had 50 communicants. Mr. Thomas died in 1706.

1703.

Pompion Hill Chapel was erected on the east side of the east branch of the Cooper. It was built of

Dalcho.

cypress, 30 feet square. The funds were contributed by Sir. N. Johnson and private subscription. The

Old Map.

Cemetery, on the original map, was 400 feet square. It was the first Church of England edifice erected outside of Charleston.

1704

The Rev. Mr. Thomas reported to the Society that the people on the eastern branch of the Cooper,

Mem. Services.

of which he had the care, numbered 80 Church and 20 dissenting families. Communicants 45; heathen slaves about 200, of whom 20 can read.

1706

St. Thomas Parish was laid off November 30, but

2 Stat. S.C. p. 282.

its boundaries were first defined December 18, 1708: " To the northeast by the bounds of Craven County; to the south by the bounds of Christ Church Parish

2 Stat. S.C. p. 329, Secs 1 and 2.

and the Wando River; to the west by the Cooper River to that tract of land commonly called the Hagin, inclusive; and to the north by the eastern branch of Cooper River to the plantation of Sir Nathaniel

Ramsay Eccles. History, page 5.

Johnson, Governor, exclusive; and then by an east line from the northmost part of said plantation to the bounds of Craven County." This was amended by an Act passed March 5, 1736-7; " bounded by the most northerly branch of the said eastern branch of the Cooper River."

The French settlement called Orange Quarter, from the principality of that name in Avignon, France, fell Shipp. within the boundaries of St. Thomas. As few of the people understood the English language, it was erected into a distinct parish, and called St. Denis, from the battlefield in the vicinity of Paris, where Admiral Coligny and the Prince of Conde met the Catholic Shipp. forces and slew their commander, Montmorenci. It was thus practically made a Church of England Parish. Hence, the people being poor, they petitioned the Assembly for the public allowance for an Episcopal minister, who should give them the English Liturgy and French sermons. The amount granted to their first missionary, Rev. John LePierre, was £20 for present relief, October 11, 1711; £50 additional, April 2, 1712; and in the next June 7, the amount was increased to £100 per annum. The church edifice was made the Chapel of Ease to the Parish Church, December 18, 1708.

The Parish Church, now called the Brick Church, 1703 about three miles from Cainhoy, on the old Clement's Ferry Road, was authorized by the Assembly, 1706. It was begun the next year and finished in 1708, which date was engraved on one of the bricks. The Glebe lands were 200 acres for the Parish Church and 420 acres for the Pompion Hill Chapel. The money allowed by the government for the Parsonage was insufficient, and placed at interest until it should amount to the sum required.

The Rev. Thomas Hasell, lately a catechist in 1709 Charleston, was appointed by the Society P. G. F. P. Humphrey. as the missionary to this Parish.

Rev. Mr. Hasell writes to the Society that he had 1711 baptized two negroes, husband and wife, and an Indian slave: all well instructed in the Christian religion; taught to read their Bible by their master and mistress, who presented them. He was very successful. The young Frenchmen who understood English constantly attended his ministry. " The books sent out by the Society to be distributed by him were of great use, especially the Common Prayer Books given to the young people of the French and to the Dissenters' children."

1713   He reported 120 families, including the French.

1714   In the old Parish Register there is the duplicate or
Old Parish
Register
copy of a Warrant on the Public Receiver for £40 : for Clerk, £10; Sexton, £5 ; Registrar, £5 ; building a south porch to the Parish Church, £18 3s. 7d. ; for the use of the poor, £1 16s. 5d. Signed, Richard Harris, Josias Dupree, Wardens ; Nathaniel Ford, Philip Chevers, Richard Smith, Peter Simons, Vestry-men ; Thomas Hasell, Rector.

1716   Mr. Hasell writes that the French desired the Lit-urgy to be translated into their own language.

1718   Vestry's warrant to Alex. Paris, Public Receiver, to
Old Parish
Register
pay the Psallary of Mr. Saville Scriven, schoolmaster of the Parish of St. Thomas, Tenne pounds.

1721   March 17.   Richard Beresford, Esq , died, and by
Dalcho.
Rivers, II.
356
Ramsay,
II., 198.
Published
Will, &c.
his will bequeathed the nett profits of his estate to the Vestry of St. Thomas Parish, in trust, until his son John, then 8 years of age, should arrive at the age of 21 years.   One-third of the interest was to be paid to schoolmasters, and two-thirds to support, maintain and educate such poor children of the parish as should be sent to the school, to learn reading, writing, casting accounts, the languages and mathematics, &c. If no school, the money to put to interest, &c.

1723   The Rev. Wm. Bull, Commissary, &c., writes to the S. P. G. : " St. Thomas is a large and populous parish. There are two churches, two glebes, but no parsonage. Rev. Mr. Hasell has been here fourteen years, resid-ing on his own estate and in a house of his own."

1728
Dalcho.
Humphrey,
103-5
The population of St. Thomas consisted of 565 whites, 950 negroes, 60 Indian slaves, 20 free negroes, or about 1600 hundred souls.

The Vestry requested the Bishop of London to send them a qualified schoolmaster.

The Rev. John LePierre, first missionary to the French, died.

Richard Harris, John Moore, Francis Goddard, John Stewart and Robert Daniel, Esq., were vestrymen, and co-defendants with the Rector and Thomas Broughton, executor, &c., in a suit by John Beresford, minor, &c., for £100 sterling, as additional allowance for his support, and £400 for his apprentice fee to Samuel Wragg, merchant, London, which he gained. *Chancery Reports.*

There was at this date a Presbyterian Church at Cainhoy, the Rev. Josias Smith, grandson of Landgrave Smith, being the minister. He removed to Charleston, and became associate pastor of the Independent Church, in 1734. The remains of this church are now called the Old Ruins. *Shipp.*

The Rev. John James Tissot was appointed missionary to St. Denis by the Bishop of London. *1730 Dalcho.*

Richard Harris, for many years Senior Warden, died, and bequeathed £500 currency, to be placed at interest until it should amount to £1000, for the education, &c., of the poor children of the parish. *1732 Dalcho. Par. Reg.*

John Beresford became of age, and the final payment of the estate completed the sum of £6500 currency, received by the Vestry. The Rev. Mr. Bull, in 1723, wrote that £150 Carolina money was equal to £120 sterling. Hence, the Beresford Endowment was originally £5200 sterling, or $26,000, and money was of greater value then than now. *1732 Ramsay, II., p. 198.*

The Vestry were incorporated, chiefly, that they might legally manage the Beresford and Harris trusts. It was the only Vestry incorporated before the Revolutionary war. The Rectors of parishes were *ex-officio* incorporated, and possessed the usual powers of corporated bodies. *1736 May 29. 3 Stat., S. C., p. 431 Colonial Church Act, Sec. xv.*

An Act was passed by the Assembly to allow the *1739*

*Act As-
sembly,
Vol. III.,
p. 516.
Ramsay,
II., 198,*

Vestry to take out of their capital stock and interest a sufficient sum for building a school.

£1200 was paid for a plantation of 600 acres, with convenient buildings, within a mile of the Parish Church. The balance of the money was placed at interest on landed security, and called the Beresford Bounty Fund. The first investment thus seems to have been in 1740, when Thomas Ashby gave a mortgage on his plantation of 500 acres for £500.

*M. C. O.
Book, v.,
p. 302.*

*1742
Sep. 21.*

The Vestry applied to the Bishop of London for an assistant to the rector (Hasell being infirm), and who might instruct the higher classes in the school, the education so far having been confined to the lower branches, as reading, writing and arithmetic.

1743

The Rev. Alexander Garden, nephew to the commissary, arrived in the parish, and was elected, July 18, the teacher of languages. Mr. Garden, also, took charge of the parish.

1744

November 9. The Rector, the Rev. Mr. Hasell, died. Had been Rector for thirty-five years. The Vestry wrote to the S. P. G. to appoint the Rev. Mr. Garden as his successor.

1747

An Act was passed declaring Pompion Hill to be the Chapel of Ease. The Rector to have service the third Sunday in each month. The Act of the Assembly, December 18, 1708, which declared St. Denis (French) to be the Chapel of Ease, was repealed.

*Dalcho.
3 Stat.,
S. C., p. 699*

*Chancery
Journal,
p. 60.*

The Vestry, by the Hon. Charles Pinckney, their solicitor, laid before the Court a copy of their accounts and proceedings under the seal of the corporation— "*Deus benedicat operi et faventi*"—down to March 25, 1747, pursuant to Act, &c.

*1750
C. Jour-
nal, p. 91.*

The same done to March 25, 1750, by the same solicitor.

1755

The Rev. Mr. Garden informed the S. P. G. that the French Refugees were dead, and their descendants, understanding English, had united themselves with the Church.

Rev. Mr. Garden had been infirm for fifteen months. 1758
Reports Church and Chapel well attended. Congre-
gations regular, serious and attentive. Had baptized
a negro child, and was preparing a negro adult for
the Lord's Supper.

He went northward for his health, and the Rev. 1760
Robert Smith, of Charleston, and the Rev. Samuel F.
Warren, of St. James, Santee, supplied services to the
parish.

April. He reports: Twenty white and one black 1762
children baptized, and that thirty are catechised every
Lord's Day.

The new chapel at Pompion Hill was begun—to be 1763
of brick, 48x35 feet—£3000 for the outside, £1000
for the inside. £200 were given by the Assembly.
Gabriel Manigault, Esq., gave £50 sterling and 960
brick tiles for the floor, valued at £10. They are in good
condition, 1884. Rev. Mr. Garden reports that the
school is flourishing. "Eight poor children are cloth-
ed, boarded and educated, i. e., taught reading, writing
and arithmetic, to fit them for apprentices. Many of
the former pupils living in the world are good Chris-
tians, and respected as sober, industrious and useful
citizens of society."

Pompion Hill Chapel was finished by private sub- 1765
scription. The architect's name, with Masonic sym-
bol, and date, are inscribed on bricks near the door.

On the death of the Rev. John James Tissot, an Act 1768
April 12.
was passed disestablishing the French Congregation
in Orange Quarter. The records, &c., lands, build- 9 Stat.,
S. C., p. 225
ings, monies, bonds and effects of said French Congregation were given to the Vestry for the benefit of
the poor of St. Thomas Parish. Among the Rules
ordered by the Vestry for the school, were :

III. The master shall bring the children to church
every Lord's Day when there is public worship, and
shall teach them to behave with all reverence while
they are in the house of God ; and to join in the

public service of the church ; for which purpose they are to be furnished with Bibles and Prayer Books as soon as they can use them.

IV.   The master shall use prayers, morning and evening, in school, and teach the children to pray, and to say grace before and after meals.

1771   March 31.   The amount of bonds at interest belonging to the Beresford Bounty Fund was £16,013 3s. 11d. currency.   Using the former proportionate value of £150 currency to £120 sterling, the amount was about £12,800 sterling, or $64,000.

1778 May 4.

Beresford Will. Pamphlet, p. 20.

The parishioners held a meeting and resolved to raise a fund for the support of an Episcopal minister and a parish clerk, and for the repairs of the Church and Chapel.

177–   The church plate was buried with that of the Rev. Robert Smith (afterwards first Bishop of South Carolina), by Mauder, his overseer, beneath a tree on his plantation. Brabant.   Mander, having been suspended

Irving, Days on Cooper River, pp. 49–57.

from the same tree three times, to force the secret of the location of the silver, in vain, was released by the British officer.   He declared that the sacredness of the communion vessels, only, restrained him from confessing.   Two cups or chalices now remain (1884), one dated 1711 ; the other 1753.   The plates are of this century.

Irving.

On Benevento plantation there was a sharp skirmish between a detachment of Marion's Brigade and a corps of Cavalry under Tarleton's command.   An old inhabitant (1843) remembers to have seen the bones of the slain whitening in the sun.   The French Quarter Creek runs between Benevento and Spring Hill plantations.

1781

Irving.

Lieut.-Col. Coates, in command of 500 infantry and 100 cavalry, was attacked by Lieut.-Col. Lee with the Legion, and Lieut.-Col. Hampton with the State cavalry.   Generals Marion and Sumter, coming up with reinforcements, continued the engagement.   The

Americans killed and wounded 40 of the British and took 140 prisoners, and a large quantity of baggage, several wagons and above 100 horses. Those who fell were buried by the roadside, from Quimby Avenue to Quimby Bridge. The Wando was the scene of many skirmishes. The British at one time fortified Cainhoy, and the Americans searched vessels passing up and down the river.

No meeting of the Vestry had been held. The funds 1779-83 were greatly reduced, as the debts were paid in paper money or "continentals."

The Rev. Alexander Garden, having been Rector 1783 for thirty-nine years, died.

By Act of the State Legislature the Vestry were 1784 allowed to sell the two glebes and purchase one more 4 Stat., central. By the same Act, the old charter was re- S. C., p. 583 newed and the former corporate powers invested in the wardens and vestrymen for the time being, and their successors. The title of St. Denis was renewed, and joined with that of St. Thomas, as one parish.

The Rev. Wm. Smith (nephew to the Bishop) was 1785 elected Rector, and continued until 1788, when he 1788 resigned.

The Rev. Samuel Nesbit became Rector. He left 1792 the State in 1793.

The Rev. George Pogson was Rector. He died of 1793 yellow fever, in Charleston, in 1794.

The Rev. John Thompson became Rector. No other 1796 record of him. He left no register.

The Rev. George T. Nankivel was Rector, and 179- served until 1809, when he returned to England. No register.

The Rev. Joseph Warren became Rector, and died 1811 in 1815. No register of his ministry extant.

An Act was passed authorizing the Vestry to dis- 1816 pose of the original school tract of land, except the 6 Stat, school-house and necessary number of acres for use. S. C., p. 42. This last was sold by the Vestry on Easter Monday,

2

1883, for about $1 per acre. The house had disappeared years ago.

1815   The Parish Church was destroyed by a fire in the woods.

1818   An Act was passed allowing the Vestry to loan the

8 Stat., S. C., p. 298   school money, in amounts, manner and security, at their discretion.

1819   The Parish Church was rebuilt, 27x37 and 22 feet high ; much smaller than the old building. No glebe. 212 white inhabitants.

1823-7   The Rev. Edward Rutledge, Rector. No register.

1827-39   The Rev. Francis H. Rutledge (afterwards Bishop of Florida), Rector. Full register.

1842-52   The Rev. Edward Philips, Rector. Register very complete.

1842   Pompion Hill Chapel. The walls threatened to

Irving, p. 63.   fall ; grass grew in the building ; the shrubbery was a wilderness ; trees grew so thickly that access to the graveyard and one of the church doors was very difficult.

1843   This year the avenue to the Chapel has been cleared,

Irving, p. 68.   the undergrowth removed, trees trimmed, and the Chapel about to be restored.

1852-3   The Rev. John H. Cornish, Rector.

1853-60   The Rev. J. Stuart Hanckel, Rector.

1856   An Act passed confirming the purchase of a lot near the village of Louisville,* for a school-house.

Stat. 12, 588.   And a general power was conferred on the Vestry to purchase property, real and personal, with the Beresford Fund, and the same to hold and resell, at their discretion, for the purposes of the charity.

1860-65   The Rev. J. Julius Sams, Rector. The Rectory near the Parish Church, occupied by the Rector, was burned by the Federal troops. A new glebe had been purchased many years before this date, and the house shortly after erected.

1867-77   The Rev. Edward C. Logan, Rector.

*Cainhoy.

A Methodist Church was organized, and a portion 1875 of the congregation of the Episcopal Church, who were dissenters, joined the movement.

An Act was passed allowing the Vestry to discon- 1878 tinue the support of children in the school, and confining their efforts to their education, until otherwise ordered by the Legislature.

April 6. The Rev. Robert F. Clute was elected 1880 Rector, including the instruction of the school children as a part his duties.

The public school, which had been connected with 1881 the Beresford school for about thirty years, was separated from the latter, on the complaint of some non-Episcopalians, who were new residents, and have since removed.

The buildings and grounds were enclosed by new 1881-3 fences. The former put in repair, and both whitewashed.

The Parish Church is in excellent condition, and 1883 outwardly, excepting the doors, is fire-proof. The graveyard is without fence, and though cleaned during the winter, is overgrown in summer with bushes. The grave-stones are in sad neglect; some fallen, some broken, all more or less covered with mould or dirt. The old vestry-room, in one corner, is probably about 175 years old. It is mentioned in R. Beresford's will, 1715, and very likely was built at the same time as the church, in 1708. The Vestry hold their Easter-meeting there. The Pompion Hill Chapel is one of the very few colonial chapels remaining as built. The floor is tiled, the seats face the aisle, the pulpit, with sounding board and prayer chancel, are are at the vestry end, and the communion chancel at the opposite end of the aisle. The building is cracked on the chancel and river sides, which will soon be repaired, but is, otherwise, in good condition. The graveyard has recently been cleaned. Some of the graves, and the first Rector's (Mr. Hasell), have disappeared into the river. In both yards many have been buried whose graves have become obliterated, and others of whom no record has been made in any register. But two families remain to attend the chapel. There are but five church families on the Wando, and they attend services at the School House Chapel. Nearly thirty white families live about Hell Hole Swamp, and twenty at Cainhoy and elsewhere. The old family residences, with very few exceptions, are going to ruin rapidly,

LIST OF MISSIONARIES AND RECTORS.

1   Rev. Mr. Corbin, Missionary,. . . 169 –1700
2   Rev. Samuel Thomas, Missionary, 1700–1706
3   Rev. Thomas Hasell, Missionary
        and Rector, ... 1709–1744† Died.
*4 Rev. John LePierre, Missionary St.
        Denis, ... 1711–1728 Died.
5   Rev. John James Tissot, Missionary
        St. Denis,. . . . . 1730–1763‡ Died.
6   Rev. Alexander Garden, Rector, . 1744–1783§ Died.
7   Rev. William Smith, Rector, . . . 1785–1788 Removed.
8   Rev. Samuel Nesbit, Rector, . . . 1792–1793 Removed.
9   Rev. George Pogson, Rector, . . . 1793–1794¶
10 Rev. John Thompson, Rector,. . . 1796   Removed.
11 Rev. George T. Nankivel, Rector, . 1806–1810 Removed.
12 Rev. Joseph Warren, Rector, . . . 1811–1815 Removed.
13 Rev. Edward Rutledge, Rector, . . 1823–1827 Removed.
14 Rev. Francis H. Rutledge, Rector, 1827–1839 Removed.
15 Rev. Edward Philips, Rector, . . . 1842–1852 Removed.
16 Rev. John H. Cornish, Rector, . . 1852–1853 Removed.
17 Rev. J. Stuart Hanckel, Rector, . . 1853–1860 Removed.
18 Rev. J. Julius Sams, Rector, . . . 1860–1865 Removed.
19 Rev. Edward C. Logan, Rector, . . 1867–1877 Removed.
20 Rev. Robert F. Clute, Rector, . . . 1880

ASSISTANT MINISTERS.

Alexander Garden,   Andrew H. Cornish,
Richard W. Seeley,   Edward C. Logan.

*Rev. Mr. Prioleau and Rev. Dr. LeJeau gave the French occasional services before the appointment of Rev. Mr LePierre as Missionary.
† B. Pompion Hill.   ‡ B. Jaudon's plantation.   § B. Charleston.
¶ B. St. Philip's, Charleston. B. Buried.

REGISTER

OF

MARRIAGES.

✝
MARRIAGES.

Marriage is honorable in all. HEB. XIII., 4.

A.

Aiken, Martha,	Monk, Thomas,	Mch. 11,	1708
Elizabeth,	Johnson, Robert,	Feb'y 1,	1759
Akins, James,	DeVeaux, Ann,	June 2,	1764
Alston, Elizabeth,	Marbeust, Joseph,	April 6,	1721
Sarah,	DuPre, Josias,	Mch. 7,	1750-1
Anne,	Waties. Thomas,	Sept. 1,	1751
Josias,	Simons, Hester,	May 26,	1752
Josias,	Proctor, Anne,	May 1,	1755
Martha,	Young, Benjamin,	June 7,	1761
Elizabeth,	Simons, Benj., Jr..	Dec'r 3,	1761
William,	Simons, Ann,	July 21,	1763
William,	Moore, Rachel,	Jan'y 19,	1775
Anderson, David,	Judon, Mary,	Nov. 25,	1756
Sarah,	Morquereau, Andrew David.	May 6,	1770
Daniel,	Dubois, Martha Esth'r	May 6,	1794
Adah,	Gyles, John,	Jan'y 20,	1875
Arthur, Christian,	Macnamara, Michael,	Nov. 29,	1726
George,	Whitesides, Sarah,	Oct. 30,	1772
Ashby, Elizabeth,	Hasell, Rev. Thomas,	Jan'y 21,	1714-5
Thomas,	LeJeau, Elizabeth,	Aug. 16,	1720
Mary,	LeJeau, Francis,	April 14,	1726
John,	Ball, Elizabeth,	Nov. 8,	1726
Ann,	Manigault, Gabriel,	April 29,	1730

Ashby,	Elizabeth,	Thomas, Samuel,	Nov.	26, 1747
	Thomas,	Bonneau, Margaret		
		Henrietta,	Dec'r	18, 1750
	John,	Bonneau, Mary,	June	10, 1755
	Ann,	Harleston, Nicholas,	Sept.	9, 1756
	Margaret,	Syme, John,	Aug.	19, 1759
	Mary,	Bochett, Lewis,	May	3, 1764
	Thomas,	Peyre, Ann,	July	15, 1772
	Eliz'th, Mrs.	Vicaridge, John,	Mch.	17
Axson,	William,	Mouzon, Elizabeth		
		Susannah,	Oct.	8, 1761

B.

Ball, Elizabeth,	Ashby, John,	Nov.	8, 1726
Ann,	Perroneau, Richard,	July	5, 1767
William,	Gibbs, Mary,	Dec.	24, 1862
Batchelor, David,	Ruberry, Sarah,	May	6, 1713
David,	Murrell, Sarah,	July	16, 1754
Baker, Michael,	Threadcroft, Mary	Sept.	7, 1727
Banbury, Peter,	Hutchinson, Charlotte,	Apl.	9, 1752
Charlotte,	Sarazin, Jonathan,	July	28, 1757
Baltezar, Joachim	Matthews, Elizabeth,	June	3, 1753
Bampfield, George,	Tart, Sarah Amelia,	Feb.	27, 1794
Barnet, Martha,	Fogartie, Joseph,	Feb.	25, 1750-1
Beresford, Mary,	King, Richard,	Apl.	26, 1709
Richard, Esq.,	Cooke, Sarah,	Jan.	4, 1711-12
Bellin, James,	Turkitt, Sarah,	Sep.	19, 1713
Bennet, John,	Hartman, Elizabeth,	Apl.	20, 1756
Thomas,	Methringham, Mary,	Dec.	2, 1765
Thomas,	Warnock, Anna,	June	9, 1774
Besselleu, Louis,	Wood, Susannah,	Aug.	27, 1775
Beaty, Ann,	Kayler, Hendrick,	Mch.	1, 1778
Beech, Mary,	Nicholas, William,	May	21, 1713
Bedon, Sarah,	Townsend, William,	Mch.	14, 1750
Bird, Thomas.	Rivers, Anne,	Apl.	19, 1753
Anne,	Cart, Joseph,	Apl.	6, 1758
Blake, Mary,	Leay, John,	Feb.	14, 1711-12

Blake, Ann,	Soulgie, John James,	June	29,	1749
Blalock, Henry,	Evans, Mary,	Jan.	1,	1829
Bona, Judith,	Jeffords, Daniel,	June	28,	1764
Bonneau, Elizabeth,	Simons, Samuel,	Dec.	4,	1724
Elias,	Miller, Susannah,	May	29,	1734
Jacob,	Miller, Mary,	Feb.	11,	1746
Elias,	Darby, Mary,	Oct.	30,	1746
Samuel,	Longuemar, Frances,	Dec.	4,	1748
Marg. Hen.	Ashby, Thomas,	Dec.	18,	1750
Hester,	Marion, Benjamin,	Nov.	22,	1752
Mary,	Ashby, John,	June	10,	1755
Rene,	Brown, John,	July	12,	1757
Hester,	Maybank, Joseph,	Dec.	16,	1759
Magdalene,	Guerin, Henry,	Dec.	5,	1760
Catharine,	Cleave, Nathan,	Aug.	13,	1763
Susannah,	Bradwell, Isaac,	Jan.	1,	1778
John Elias,	Phillips, Martha,	Mch.	11,	1846
Bochett, Henry,	Jennens, Ann,	Aug.	13,	1746
Elizabeth,	Mouzon, Lewis, Jr.,	June	13,	1750
Peter,	DuBois, Frances,	June	—,	1751
Anthony,	Mouzon, Hester,	May	9,	1754
Anthony,	Scott, Mary,	Nov.	7,	1759
Lewis,	Ashby, Mary,	May	3,	1764
Frances,	Guerin, Samuel,	Mch.	3,	1774
Mary,	Taylor, William,	Nov.	14,	1776
Boyneau, Michael, of Santee,	Sanders, Elizabeth,	Sep.	13,	1764
Bonny, Thomas,	Walblank, Ruth,	Sep.	14,	1721
Ann,	Hull, William,	May	1,	1745
Bond, Geo. Padon,	Padgett, Constantia,	June	11,	1752
Hester,	Rose, John,	Oct.	10,	1754
Boyd, Robert,	Walker, Anne,	Sep.	19,	1762
Boisseau, Catharine,	Dubois, Isaac,	July	9,	1749
Bourdeaux, Elizab'h,	Dearington, Thomas,	May	25,	1766
Esther,	Stinson, Thomas,	May	19,	1768
Bollard, Mary Chris'n	Eddie, James,	Dec.	18,	1751
Bradwell, Isaac,	Bonneau, Susannah,	Jan'y	1,	1778
Brockenton, William,	Griffen, Sarah,	July	5,	1715

Bremar, Martha,	Scriven, Saville,	Apl.	29, 1718
Peter,	Shekelford, Elizabe'h,	May	9, 1718
James,	Shekelford,Vollentine,	Feby.	4, 1722-3
Elizabeth,	LeBruce, Joseph,	July	3, 1744
Mary,	Marion, James,	Apl.	13, 1749
Brown, Alexander,	Dutarque, Mary,	Aug.	16, 1744
John.	Bonneau, Rene,	July	12, 1757
Rene,	Miller, William,	Sep.	13, 1763
Hannah,	Simons, Anthony,	Sep.	16, 1775
Bruce, John,	Sanders, Ann,	Feb.	14, 1750-1
Priscilla,	Hall, Thomas,	Oct.	25, 1753
Breckenrige, Adam,	Carwithin, Ann,	July	7, 1755
Brindley, John Geo.,	Jeffords, Sarah,	June	18, 1767
Esther,	Stewart, Charles,	June	16, 1794
Brabant, Jean,	DuPre, Cornelius,	Nov.	20, 1708
Brownluff, Hannah,	Lewis, James,	July	29, 1746
Burdell, Jacob,	Carrier, Elizabeth,	Feb.	18, 1713 4
John,	McGrigor, Elizabeth,	Apl.	17, 1748
Bunch, Margaret,	Mitchell, Ambrose,	Jany.	4, 1829
Burley, Richard,	Scott, Frances,	Apl.	12, 1750
Buttler, Thomas,	Lunberry, Elizabeth,	July	5, 1767
Thomas,	Miller, Mary,	Oct.	7, 1773
Burrows, Richard.	McCulloch, Mary,	Feb.	18, 1770
Bullock, Mary,	Elliot, John,	Mch.	31, 1757
Samuel,	Hales, Rhoda,	July	12, 1770
Burnham, Mary,	Cooke, Edward,	Nov.	30, 1750

C.

Capers, William,	Dutarque, Catharine,	Dec.	4, 1753
Cart, Joseph,	Bird, Anne,	Apl.	6, 1758
Joseph,	Walker, Martha,	Dec.	14, 1760
Cape, Brian,	Hetherington, Mary,	May	6, 1770
Canty, Elizabeth,	Russ, Abijah,	Apl.	6. 1758
Carrier, Elizabeth,	Burdell, Jacob,	Feb.	18. 1713-4
Carwithin, Ann,	Breckenrige, Adam,	July	7, 1755
Chovin, Alexander,	Tart, Mary,	Nov.	12, 1772
Chappel, Amelia,	Munro, Barnabas,	Apl.	2, 1776

Chapley,	McDole,	May	4,	1732
Chicken, Catharine,	Simons, Benj'n, Jr.,	Sept.	27,	1764
Clyatt, Robert,	Stone, Hannah,	July	28,	1713
Clerk, Joseph,	Tyran, Anna,	Mch.	25,	1725
Cleave, Nathan,	Sanders, Hannah,	Aug.	27,	1761
Nathan,	Bonneau, Catharine,	Aug.	13,	1763
Catharine,	Peyre, Rene,	July	18,	1765
Commander, Thomas,	Griffen, Sarah,	Apl.	1,	1713
Conyears, John,	Quarterman, Mary,	July	15,	1717
Cordes, Hester,	Dwight, Rev. Daniel,	Apl.	21,	1747
Thomas,	Ravenell, Ann,	July	6,	1749
Cooke, Sarah,	Beresford, Richard,	Jany.	4,	1711-2
Edward,	Burnham, Mary,	Nov.	30,	1750
Collings, Jonathan,	Simons, Anne,	Jany.	3,	1743-4
Jonathan,	McGrigory, Mary,	Oct.	20,	1745
Sarah,	Don, Peter,	Oct.	16,	1764
Combe, Martha,	Murrell, Robert,	Apl.	2,	1749
John,	, Jane,	Nov.	23,	1751
Collins, Maryan,	Luyten, William,	May	29,	1764
Codner, Sabina,	Rows, James,	May	25,	1724
Crouch, Sarah,	Danzy, Richard,	Oct.	2,	1723
Cromwell, Jemima,	Murrell, Robert,	Nov.	3,	1763
Cusack, Adam,	Oran, Frances,	Sept.	13,	1764
Cuming, Anne,	Rochford, James,	Dec.	5,	1751

D.

Daniel, Robert,	Perryman, Elizabeth,	Jany.	7,	1721-2
Anna,	Goodbie, Alexander,	Dec.	9,	1725
— widow,	Tresvin, William.	July	17,	1734
Robert,	Russ, Elizabeth,	Dec,	19,	1754
Darby, Mary,	Bonneau, Elias,	Oct.	30,	1746
Michael,	Warnock, Mary,	May	21,	1717
Danzy, Richard,	Crouch, Sarah,	Oct.	2,	1723
Dallas, Walter,	Padgett, Judith,	June	8,	1727
Davis, Joseph,	White, Mary,	July	10,	1754
Dannelly, Edward,	Sanders, Patience,	Feb.	5,	1756
Dewitt, Ann,	Simons, Benj'n,	Mch.	13,	1755

Dearington, Thomas,	Bourdeaux, Eliz'th,	May	25, 1766
John,	Simons, Elizabeth,	May	24, 1772
Deveaux, Ann,	Aikins, James,	June	2, 1764
Mary Caroline,	Withers, Thomas,	Apl.	8, 1778
Dickson, Spartan C.,	Muirhead, Rosa E. Mrs.	Feb.	10, 1875
Don, Peter,	Collings, Sarah,	Oct.	16, 1764
Doorne, Hannah,	Lodge, John,	Feb.	10, 1778
Drake, Elizabeth,	Ellis, Thomas,	Feb.	18, 1744-5
Edward,	Ruberry, Ann,	Apl.	1753
DuPre, Cornelius,	Brabant, Jean,	Nov.	20, 1708
Josias,	Alston, Sarah,	Mch.	7, 1750-1
Dubois, Isaac,	Boisseau, Catharine,	July	9, 1749
Frances,	Bochett, Peter,	June	1751
Peter,	Mouzon, Ann,	June	11, 1752
John,	Mouzon, Sarah,	Nov.	16, 1758
James,	Guerin, Hester,	Dec.	11, 1760
Hester,	Guerin, Vincent,	Aug.	19, 1773
Frances,	Wells, William,	Oct.	20, 1774
Susannah,	Plowden, William,	July	24, 1777
Martha Est'r,	Anderson, Daniel,	May	6, 1794
Dutarque, Esther,	Fogartie, Stephen,	May	9, 1721
Mary,	Brown, Alexander,	Aug.	16, 1744
Martha,	Miller, Stephen,	June	19, 1746
John, Jr.,	Serre, Mary,	Feb.	6, 1753
Catharine,	Capers, William,	Dec.	4, 1753
Hester,	Joel, Thomas,	May	22, 1763
Mary,	Jennings, John,	Jany.	20, 1765
Martha,	Wigfall, Benjamin,	Aug.	1, 1771
Dutart, Ella, M.,	Freeman. John T.	Nov.	4, 1875
Duke, Elizabeth,	Simons, Henry,	Jany.	28, 1766
Mary,	Frasier, John,	Aug.	8, 1771
Duberdeaux, Mrs.,	Mouzon, Lewis, Jr.,	Oct.	17, 1731
Durand, Susannah,	Wigfall, Joseph,	Nov.	3, 1768
Dwight, Daniel, Rev.	Cordes, Hester,	Apl.	21, 1747
Dysart, George,	Martin, Hannah,	May	4, 1732

E.

Edwards, Edward,	Syer, Mary,	Sep.	25, 1772
Eddie, James,	Bollard, Mary Chris'n,	Dec.	18, 1751
Eden, Jeremiah,	Rouser, Sarah,	Mch.	26, 1761
Edon, Mary,	Litz, Bernard,	Mch.	31, 1754
Ellis, Thomas,	Drake, Elizabeth,	Feb.	18, 1744-5
Samuel,	Vanal, Hester,	Aug.	12, 1770
Elliott, John,	Bullock, Mary,	Mch.	31, 1757
Elder, Thomas,	Hartley, Charlotte,	May	6, 1773
Ellery, Anne,	Pawley, George,	Jany.	26, 1748-9
Elfe, Emily W.,	Ward, John,	Mch.	21, 1871
Ettering, Margaret,	Welsh, George,	Aug.	6, 1767
Evans, Elias,	Mordah, Mary,	Dec.	27, 1772
Evans, Mary,	Blalock, Henry,	Jany.	1, 1829

F.

Finlayson, Mungo,	Hartley, Mary Ann,	Mch.	20, 1869
Fitch, Mary,	Livingston, William,	Sep.	1, 1747
Follingsby, Jane,	Vanderhorst, Joseph,	May	14, 1758
Ford, Nathaniel,	King, Mary, Mrs.	May	6, 1714
Joseph,	Turkitt, Mary,	Mch.	5, 1716-7
Sarah,	Horrey, Daniel,	Jany	12, 1743-4
Fogartie, Stephen,	Dutarque, Esther,	May	9, 1721
David,	Nailor, Mary,	July	20, 1749
Joseph,	Barnet, Martha,	Feb.	25, 1750-1
David,	Green, Rebecca,	May	2, 1759
James,	Garden, Marg't Ame'a,	Aug.	25, 1776
Dutart,	Seely, Eliza A., Mrs.,	Dec.	11, 1828
Louisa,	Poyas, John L.,	Nov.	25, 1829
Frewin, Charles,	Simons, Ann,	Feb.	10, 1767
Frasier, John,	Duke, Mary,	Aug.	8, 1771
Fewelling, Deborah,	Singletarry Braton,	Dec,	15, 1711
Freeman, John T.,	Dutart, Ella M.,	Nov.	4, 1875

G.

Garden, Alex., Rev.,	Hartley, Amey,	Dec.	14, 1749
Elizabeth,	Tart, Nathan,	Mch.	31, 1771
Margaret A.,	Fogartie, James,	Aug,	25, 1776
Gabeau, Anne, E.,	Hamlin, Edward,	Apl.	4, 1850
Gilmore, John,	Hartman, Eliz'th,	May	28, 1775
Gibbes, William,	Hasell, Elizabeth,	Feb.	18, 1747
Gibbs, Mary,	Ball, Wm. (Limerick),	Dec.	24, 1862
Glen, William,	Miller, Martha,	Apl.	12, 1770
Goodbie, John	Wallbank, Hannah,	Dec.	29, 1713
Alexander,	Daniel, Anna,	Dec.	9, 1725
Elizabeth,	Hayes, Charles,	May	12, 1730
Goddard, Francis,	Manwaring, Mary,	Jany.	14, 1713-4
Green, William,	Thompson, Jane,	July	17, 1752
Rebecca,	Fogartie, David,	May	2, 1759
Grange, Sarah,	Moor, Nathaniel,	Apl.	13, 1720
Gray, Ann,	Simons, Benj. of Sewee,	Sept.	4, 1766
Griffen, Sarah,	Commander, Thomas,	Apl.	1, 1713
Sarah,	Brockenton, William,	July	5, 1715
Guerin, Vincent,	Guerin, Judith,	July	12, 1703
Judith,	Guerin, Vincent,	July	12, 1703
Elizabeth,	How, Robert,	July	3, 1729
Isaac,	Mouzon, Martha,	Apl.	15, 1730
Marian,	Roulain, Abraham,	Dec.	6, 1733
John,	Johnston, Eliz'th,	May	20, 1746
Elisha,	Kelly, Lucretia,	Oct.	29, 1749
Peter,	Norman, Mary Ann,	Jany.	4, 1749-50
Elizabeth,	Singletarry, Thomas,	Feb.	22, 1759
Robert,	Sanders, Sarah,	July	12, 1759
Henry,	Bonneau, Magdalene,	Dec.	5, 1760
Hester,	Dubois, James,	Dec.	11, 1760
Martha,	Jaudon, Paul,	Jany.	5, 1772
Vincent,	Dubois, Hester,	Aug.	19, 1773
Samuel,	Bochett, Frances,	Mch.	3, 1774
Guthrie, Elizabeth,	Matthews, John,	July	25, 1749
Guyton, Mary,	Sloan, Allen,	June	7, 1837
Gyles, John,	Anderson, Adah,	Jany	20, 1875

H.

Hasell, Thomas, Rev.,	Ashby, Elizabeth,	Jany.	21, 1714-5
Thomas,	Morrit, Alice,	Apl.	26, 1744
Elizabeth,	Gibbes, William,	Feb.	18, 1747
John,	Simons, Hannah,	Apl.	27, 1749
Andrew,	Wigfall, Sarah,	Mch.	28, 1751
Hannah,	Peyre, Rene,	Dec.	9, 1753
Constantia,	Quash, Robert,	May	17, 1772
Hales, Rhoda,	Bullock, Sam'l,	July	12, 1770
John,	Rupp, Margaret,	Dec.	23, 1777
Hamilton, Archibald,	Roche, Bridget,	Jany.	10, 1726-7
Hayes, Charles,	Goodbie, Eliz'th,	May	12, 1730
Hall, Thomas,	Bona Priscilla,	Oct.	25, 1753
Priscilla,	Tart, Nathan,	Dec.	3, 1758
Grace,	Jervey, Thomas,	July	22, 1770
Harleston, Nicholas,	Ashby, Anne,	Sep.	9, 1756
Hartley, Amey,	Garden, Alex., Rev.,	Dec.	14, 1749
Magd. Eliz.,	Warnock, Sam'l,	June	12, 1755
Rebecca,	Withers, William,	Nov.	27, 1755
Mary Ann,	Finlayson, Mungo,	Mch.	20, 1769
Charlotte,	Elder, Thomas,	May	6, 1773
Hartman, Elizabeth,	Bennet, John,	Apl.	20, 1756
Mary,	Rouser, William,	May	31, 1756
Elizabeth,	Gilmore, John,	May	28, 1775
Hamlin, Sam'l W.,	McDowell, Sarah, E.,	Nov.	25, 1829
Mary G.,	Lachicotte, Julius,	May	15, 1833
Eliza,	McDowell, Geo. A.,	Oct.	24, 1833
Susan T.,	McDowell, Wm. B.,	Nov.	5, 1835
Edward,	Gabeau, Anne E.,	Apl.	4, 1850
Theodore T.,	Poyas, Sarah R.,	Apl.	28, 1874
Henly, Sarah,	Law, Joseph,	Jany.	1, 1754
Heatley, Richard,		Nov.	5, 1714
Heskett, John,	Russ, Martha,	Mch.	2, 1762
Hetherington, John,	Miller, Mary,	Aug.	16, 1763
Mary,	Cape, Brian,	May	6, 1770
Hearin, Zacheriah,	Manduvel, Margaret,	Aug.	29, 1775
Houscausen, Odelia,	Miller, Jacob,	Apl.	12, 1748

3

Howard, Sarah,	Wright, William,	Mch. 19, 1711-12
Margaret,	Jeffers, John,	Aug. 12, 1714
Edward,	Jones, Letties,	Sep. 23, 1716
Anna,	June, John,	Mch. 5, 1718-9
Edward,	St. Martin, Ann,	Mch. 28, 1727-8
How, Robert,	Guerin, Elizabeth,	July 3, 1729
Howe, Martha Jane,	Logan, Daniel W., (Mobile),	July 15, 1872
Hood, Jesse,	White, Mar'e Susan'h,	Dec. 28, 1855
Horrey, Eliz'th Mary,	Lewis, Charles,	Aug. 8, 1713
Mary,	Laroche, John,	Aug. 28, 1714
Magdalen,	Trapier, Paul,	Sep. 22, 1743
Daniel,	Ford Sarah,	Jan. 12, 1743-4
Hutchinson, Charl'e,	Banbury, Peter,	Apl. 9, 1752
Hull, William,	Bonny, Ann,	May 1, 1745
Huger, Daniel,	LeJeau, Anne,	Oct. 18, 1749
Hume, Robert,	Quash, Susannah,	Apl. 24, 1766
Susannah,	Pinckney, Roger,	Mch. 26, 1769

I.

Irons, Stephen,	Rupp, Barbara,	Aug. 6, 1777
I'Ons, Susannah,	Rose, John,	Apl. 14, 1778

J.

Jaudon, James,	Pedriau, Mary,	Feb. 9, 1769
Paul,	Guerin, Martha,	Jany. 5, 1772
Jeffers, John,	Howard, Margaret,	Aug. 12, 1714
Jefferds, Ann,	Miller, Moses,	Aug. 20, 1747
John,	Miller, Magdalen,	June 1, 1749
Jeffords, Daniel,	Bona, Judith,	June 28, 1764
Sarah,	Brindley, John Geo.,	June 18, 1767
Jenkins, Thomas,	Johnson, Mary,	Mch. 30, 1719
Jennings, Elizabeth,	Pring, William,	Sep. 2, 1747
Mary,	Micheau, Daniel,	Apl. 6, 1756
John,	Dutarque, Mary,	Jany. 20, 1765
Jennens, Ann,	Bochett, Henry,	Aug. 13, 1746

Jervey, Thomas,	Hall, Grace,	July 22, 1770
Johnston, Elizabeth,	Guerin, John,	May 20, 1746
Robert,	Aiken, Elizabeth,	Feb. 1, 1759
Richard,	Thomson, Rebecca,	Mch. 23, 1761
Johnson, Mary,	Jenkins, Thomas,	Mch. 30, 1719
Mary,	King, Charles,	Feb. 13, 1732
Joel, Thomas,	Dutarque, Hester,	May 22, 1763
Jones, Letties,	Howard, Edward,	Sep. 23, 1716
June, John,	Howard, Anna,	Mch. 5, 1718-9
Solomon,	Stanley, Anna,	May 30, 1727
Judon, Mary,	Anderson, David,	Nov. 25, 1756

K.

Karwon, Thomas,	Marion, Mary,	Jany. 3, 1773
Kayler, Mary,	Sharp, Alexander,	Feb. 11, 1776
Henrick,	Beaty, Ann,	Mch. 1, 1778
King, Samuel,	Preston, Elizabeth,	May 17, 1706
Richard,	Beresford, Mary,	Apl. 26, 1709
Mary, Mrs.,	Ford, Nathaniel,	May 6, 1714
Robert,	Marbeust, Hannah,	Dec. 29, 1714
Mary,	Musgrove, John,	Feb. 24, 1729
Charles,	Johnson, Mary,	Feb. 13, 1732
Ann,	Whilden, Jonathan,	Dec. 19, 1749
George,	Mahan, Elizabeth,	Oct. 22, 1752

L.

Laroche, John,	Horrey, Mary,	Aug. 28, 1714
Law, Joseph,	Henley, Sarah,	Jany. 17, 1754
Lachicotte, Julius,	Hamlin, Mary G.,	May 15, 1833
Lewis, Charles,	Horrey, Eliz'th Mary,	Aug. 8, 1713
Mary,	McDaniel, Daniel,	June 4, 1723
James,	Brownluff, Hannah,	July 29, 1746
Lesesne, Isaac,	Netherton, Frances,	Aug. 30, 1722
Daniel,	Simons, Mary,	Jany. 22, 1756
Sarah,	Parker, William,	Dec. 25, 1760
Elizabeth,	Scott, Joseph,	June 14, 1761

Lejeau, Elizabeth,	Ashby, Thomas,	Aug. 16, 1720
Francis,	Ashby, Mary,	Apl. 14, 1726
. Anne,	Huger, Daniel,	Oct. 18, 1749
Leay, John,	Blake, Mary,	Feb. 14, 1711–2
LeBruce, Joseph,	Bremar, Elizabeth,	July 3, 1744
Legare, Daniel,	Redford, Elizabeth,	Jany. 1, 1753
Leroux, John,	Vanall, Elizabeth,	June 26, 1757
Littenwere, ——	Russ, Jonathan,	Feb. 26, 1721–2
Livingston, William,	Fitch, Mary,	Feb. 1, 1747
Litz, Barnard,	Edon, Mary,	Mch. 31, 1754
Lodge, John,	Doorne, Hannah,	Feb. 10, 1778
Longuemar, Frances,	Bonneau, Samuel,	Dec. 4, 1748
Logan, Dan'l W. (Mobile),	Howe, Martha Jane,	July 15, 1872
Luyten, William,	Collins, Maryan,	May 29, 1764
Lunberry, Elizabeth,	Butler, Thomas,	July 5, 1767

M.

Manigault, Gabriel,	Ashby, Ann,	Apl. 29, 1730
Marion, James,	Bremar, Mary,	Apl. 13, 1749
Benjamin,	Bonneau, Hester,	Nov. 22, 1752
John,	Sanders, Mary,	Feb. 14, 1760
Mary,	Karwon, Thomas,	Jany. 3, 1773
Marbeust, Hannah,	King, Robert,	Dec. 29, 1714
Joseph,	Alston, Elizabeth,	Apl. 6, 1721
Maxwell, James,	Simons, Mary,	Sep. 7, 1722–3
Matthews, John,	Guthrie, Elizabeth,	July 24, 1749
Elizabeth,	Baltezar, Joachim,	June 3, 1753
Maybank, Joseph,	Bonneau, Hester,	Dec. 16, 1759
Martin, Hannah,	Dyzart, George,	May 4, 1732
Edward,	Walker, Elizabeth,	Jany. 20, 1763
Elizabeth,	Mosse, George,	Oct. 30, 1767
William,	Williams, Leah,	Nov. 25, 1777
Samuel,	Phillips, Eliza,	Dec. 19, 1843
Manwaring, Mary,	Goddard, Francis,	Jany. 14, 1713–4
Manduvel, Margaret,	Hearim, Zachariah,	Aug. 29, 1775
Mahan, Elizabeth,	King, George,	Oct. 22, 1752

Macnamara, Michael,	Arthur, Christian,	Nov. 29, 1726
Maculloch, Mary,	Burrows, Richard,	Feb. 18, 1770
McDaniel, Daniel,	Lewis, Mary,	June 4, 1723
McDole,	Chapley,	May 4, 1732
McDowell, Sarah E.,	Hamlin, Samuel W.,	Nov. 25, 1829
George A..	Hamlin, Eliza,	Oct. 24, 1833
William B.,	Hamlin, Susan T.,	Nov. 5, 1835
McGrigory, Mary,	Collings, Jonathan,	Oct. 20, 1745
Elizabeth,	Burdell, John,	Apl. 17, 1748
Elizabeth,	Simons, Francis,	May 29, 1750
Metheringham, Mary,	Bennet, Thomas,	Dec. 2, 1765
Miller, Susannah,	Bonneau, Elias,	May 29, 1734
Mary,	Bonneau, Jacob,	Feb. 11, 1746
Stephen,	Dutarque, Martha,	June 19, 1746
Moses,	Jeffords, Ann,	Aug. 20, 1747
Jacob,	Houscausen, Odelia,	Apl. 12, 1748
Magdalen,	Jeffords, John,	June 1, 1749
Mary,	Pawley, George,	May 22, 1755
Mary,	Hetherington, John,	Aug. 16, 1763
William,	Brown, Rene,	Sept. 13, 1763
Martha,	Glen, William,	Apl. 12, 1770
Stephen,	Roche, Mary,	Sept. 27, 1770
Mary,	Buttler, Thomas,	Oct. 7. 1773
Millikan, Moses,	Murrell, Mary,	Sept. 9, 1721
Micheau, Daniel,	Jennings, Mary,	Apl. 6, 1756
Mills, Anna, Mrs.	Songster, Andrew,	Oct. 21, 1721
Mitchell, Ambrose,	Bunch, Margaret,	Jany. 4, 1829
Mouzon, Martha,	Guerin, Isaac,	Apl. 15, 1731
Lewis, Jr.,	Duberdeaux, —, Mrs,,	Oct. 17, 1731
Lewis, Jr.,	Bochett, Elizabeth,	June 13, 1750
Ann,	Dubois, Peter,	June 11, 1752
Hester,	Bochett, Anthony,	May 9, 1754
Sarah,	Dubois, John,	Nov. 16, 1758
Elizabeth S.,	Axson, William,	Oct. 8, 1761
Mary Ann,	Sanders, Thos. Martin,	May 16, 1764
Moor, Nathaniel,	Grange, Sarah,	Apl. 13, 1720
Moore, Rachel,	Alston, William,	Jany 19, 1775
Mosse, George,	Martin, Elizabeth,	Oct. 30, 1767

Morquereau, And. D.,	Anderson, Sarah,	May	6, 1770
Mordah, Mary,	Evans, Elias,	Dec.	27, 1772
Morritt, Alice,	Hasell, Thomas,	Apl.	26, 1744
Motte, Elizabeth,	Simons, Francis,	Apl	30, 1767
Morrenna, Magdalen,	Threadcroft, Thomas,	July	15, 1745
Monk, Thomas,	Aiken, Martha,	Mch.	11, 1708
Murrel, Mary,	Millikan, Moses,	Sept.	9, 1721
Robert,	Combe, Martha,	Apl.	2, 1749
Sarah,	Batchelor, David,	July	16, 1754
Susannah,	Whilden, John,	Feb.	20, 1755
Robert,	Cromwell, Jemima,	Nov.	3, 1763
Musgrove, John,	King, Mary,	Feb.	24, 1729
Munro, Barnabas,	Chappell, Amelia,	Apl.	2, 1776
Muirhead, Rosa,			
E., Mrs.,	Dickson, Spartan C.,	Feb.	10, 1875

N.

Nailor, Mary,	Forgartie, David,	July	20, 1749
Naylor, John,	Poitevin, Mary,	Nov.	30, 1742
Neufville, Isaac,	Simons, Ann,	Apl.	5, 1794
Nicholas, William,	Beech, Mary,	May	21, 1713
Norman, Mary Ann,	Guerin, Peter,	Jany.	4, 1749-50

O.

Oran, Frances,	Cusack, Adam,	Sep.	13, 1764

P.

Parker, William,	Lesesne, Sarah,	Dec.	26, 1760
Pawley, George,	Ellery, Anne,	Jany.	26, 1748-9
George,	Miller, Mary,	May	22, 1755
Pagett, Constantia,	Bond, George Padon,	June	11, 1752
Padgitt, Judith,	Dallas, Walter,	June	3, 1727
Palthezar, Elizabeth,	Smith, John,	Jany.	12, 1760
Paris, Elizabeth,	Withers, Richard,	Apl.	10, 1755
Peyre, Rene,	Hasell, Hannah,	Dec.	9, 1753

Peyre, Rene,	Cleave, Catharine,	July	18, 1765
Ann,	Ashby, Thomas,	July	15, 1772
Perroneau, Richard,	Ball, Ann,	July	5, 1767
Peacock, Thomas,	Room, Anna, Mrs.,	Feb.	24, 1718–9
Perryman, Elizabeth,	Daniel, Robert,	Jany.	7, 1721–2
Pedriau, Mary,	Jaudon, James,	Feb.	9, 1769
Phillips, Eliza,	Martin, Samuel,	Dec.	19, 1843
Martha,	Bonneau, John E.,	Mch.	11, 1846
Pinckney, Roger,	Hume, Susannah		
	Quash, Mrs.	Mch.	26, 1769
Hopson,	Quash, Elizabeth,	Nov.	19, 1772
Plumer, Moses,	Verine. Jean, Mrs.	Feb.	15, 1712–3
Plowden, William,	Dubois, Susannah,	July	24, 1777
Poole, William,	Warbeuf, Hannah,	Dec.	8, 1726
Poitevin, Susannah,	Snow, John,	Oct.	4, 1720
Mary,	Naylor, John,	Nov.	30, 1742
Hester,	Snow, Nathaniel,	Aug.	5, 1750
Susannah,	Snow, John,	Feb.	16, 1762
Pollock, Marg't. Mrs.	Vanderhost, John,	Sep.	8, 1714
Poyas, John L.,	Fogartie, Louisa, Mrs.,	Nov.	25, 1829
Mary Magd'n,	Sanders, William,	Jany.	10, 1850
Louisa Ann,	Tiencken, John,	May	21, 1873
Sarah R.,	Hamlin, Theodore T.,	Apl.	28, 1874
Pring, William,	Jennings, Elizabeth,	Sep.	2, 1747
Proctor, Anne,	Alston, Josias,	May	1, 1755
Preston, Elizabeth,	King, Samuel,	May	17, 1706
Purry, Francis,	Sallens, Freelove, Mrs.,	May	9, 1728

Q.

Quash, Susannah,	Hume, Robert,	Apl.	24, 1766
Sus'h H., wid			
R. Hume,	Pinckney, Roger,	Mch.	26, 1769
Robert,	Hasell, Constantia,	May	17, 1772
Elizabeth,	Pinckney, Hopson,	Nov.	19, 1772
Quarterman, Mary,	Conyears, John,	July	15, 1717

R.

Ravenell, Ann,	Cordes, Thomas,	July 6, 1749
Redford, Elizabeth,	Legare, Daniel,	Jany. 1, 1753
Rivers, Morrice,	Savige, Margaret,	Aug. 9, 1722
Anne,	Bird, Thomas,	Apl. 19, 1753
Roper, Lidia,	Wells, Edger,	June 29, 1709
Jeremiah,	Warnock, Mary,	Dec. 8, 1711
Rows, James,	Codner, Sabina, Mrs.,	May 25, 1724
Rolang, Abraham,	Guerin, Marian,	Dec. 6, 1733
Rochford, James,	Cuming, Anne,	Dec. 5, 1751
Rose, John,	Bond, Hester,	Oct. 10, 1754
John,	I'On, Susannah,	Apl. 14, 1778
Roddam, Sarah,	White, John,	Aug. 6, 1774
Rouser, William,	Hartman, Mary,	May 31, 1756
Sarah,	Eden, Jeremiah,	Mch. 26, 1761
Roche, Bridget,	Hamilton, Archibald,	Jany. 10, 1726-7
Mary,	Miller, Stephen,	Sep. 27, 1770
Room, Anna, Mrs.,	Peacock, Thomas,	Feb. 24, 1718-9
Russ, Jonathan,	Littlewere, ——,	Feb 26, 1721-2
David,	—— Catharine,	Nov. 2, 1722
Elizabeth,	Daniel, Robert,	Dec. 19, 1754
Abijah,	Canty, Elizabeth,	Apl. 6, 1758
Martha,	Heskett, John,	Mch. 2, 1762
Ruberry, Sarah,	Batchelor, David,	May 6, 1713
Anne,	Drake, Edward,	Apl. —, 1753
Rupp, Barbara,	Irons, Stephen,	Aug. 6, 1777
Margaret,	Hales, John,	Dec. 23, 1777

S.

Sanders, Sarah,	Tart, Nathan,	May 7, 1747
Ann,	Bruce, John,	Feb. 14, 1750-1
Patience,	Dannelly, Edward,	Feb. 5, 1756
Sarah,	Guerin, Robert,	July 12, 1759
Mary,	Marion, John,	Feb. 14, 1760
Hannah,	Cleave, Nathan,	Aug. 27, 1761

Sanders, Elizabeth,	Boyneau, Michael, of Santee,	Sep.	13,	1764
William,	Poyas, Mary Magd'n,	Jan.	10,	1850
Mary, Mrs.	Ward, I. M.,	Sep.	5,	1859
Saunders, John,	St. Martin, Mary,	May	9,	1727
Thomas Martin,	Mouzon, Mary Ann,	May	16,	1764
Thomas Martin,	Thomas, Elizabeth,	Jany,	8,	1767
Sarazin, Jonathan,	Banbury, Charlotte,	July	28,	1757
Sallens, Freelove, Mrs.	Purry, Francis,	May	9,	1728
Savige, Margaret,	Rivers, Morrice,	Aug.	9,	1722
Scriven, Saville,	Bremar, Martha,	Apl.	29,	1718
Martha, Mrs.,	Tresvan, Theodorus,	Feb.	24,	1720-1
Scott, Frances,	Burley, Richard,	Apl.	12,	1750
Mary,	Bockett, Anthony,	Nov.	7,	1759
Joseph,	Lesesne, Elizabeth,	June	14,	1761
Serre, Mary,	Dutarque, John, Jr.,	Feb.	6,	1753
Seely, Eliza A.,	Fogartie, Dutart,	Dec.	11,	1828
Sharp, Alex'r,	Kayler, Mary,	Feb.	11,	1776
Shekelford, Elizab'h,	Bremar, Peter,	May	9,	1718
Vollentine,	Bremar, James,	Feb.	4,	1722-3
Simons, Mary,	Maxwell, James,	Sep.	7,	1723
Samuel,	Bonneau, Elizabeth,	Dec.	4,	1724
Martha,	Young, Archibald,	Nov.	22,	1726
Anne,	Collings, Jonathan,	Jany.	3,	1743-4
Elizabeth,	Vanderhorst, Arnoldus,	July	18,	1745
Hannah,	Hasell, John,	Apl.	27,	1749
Francis,	McGrigory, Elizabeth,	May	29,	1750
Hester,	Alston, Josias,	May	26,	1752
Benjamin,	Dewitt, Ann,	Mch.	13,	1755
Mary,	Lesesne, Daniel,	Jany,	22,	1756
Benj'n, Jr.,	Alston, Elizabeth,	Dec.	3,	1761
Ann,	Alston, William,	July	21,	1763
Benj'n, Jr.,	Chicken, Catharine,	Sep.	27,	1764
Henry,	Duke, Elizabeth,	Jany.	28,	1766
Ben. of Sewee,	Gray, Ann,	Sep.	4,	1766
Ann,	Frewin, Charles,	Feb.	10,	1767
Francis,	Motte, Elizabeth,	Apl.	30,	1767
Anthony,	Brown, Hannah,	Sep.	16,	1775

Simons, Ann,	Neufville, Isaac,	Apl.	5, 1794
Singletarry, Braton,	Fewelling, Deborah,	Dec.	15, 1711
Thomas,	Guerin, Elizabeth,	Feb.	22, 1759
Skinner, Joseph,	——, Catharine,	Jany.	28, 1741
Sloan, Allen,	Guyton, Mary,	June	7, 1837
Smith, John,	Palthezar, Elizabeth,	Jany.	12, 1760
Snow, John,	Poitevin, Susannah,	Oct.	4, 1720
Nathaniel,	Poitevin, Hester,	Aug.	5, 1750
John,	Poitevin, Susannah,	Feb.	16, 1762
Songster, Andrew,	Mills, Anna, Mrs.,	Oct.	21, 1721
Soulegre, John Jas.,	Blake, Anne,	June	29, 1749
St. Martin, Mary,	Saunders, John,	May	9, 1727
Ann,	Howard, Edward,	May	28, 1728
Stone, Hannah,	Clyatt, Robert,	July	28, 1713
Joseph,	——, Mary,	Apl.	18, 1723
Stinson, Thomas,	Bourdeaux, Esther,	May	19, 1768
Stewart, Charles,	Brindley, Esther,	June	16, 1794
Stanley, Elizabeth,	Witten, Thomas,	Aug.	15, 1718
Anna,	June, Solomon,	May	30, 1727
Syme, John,	Ashby, Margaret,	Aug	19, 1759
Syer, Mary,	Edwards, Edward,	Sep.	25, 1772

T.

Taylor, Susannah,	Watts, Thomas,	Oct.	12, 1756
William,	Bochett, Mary,	Nov.	14, 1776
Thomas, Sam'l, Rev.,	Ashby, Elizabeth,	Nov.	26, 1747
Elizabeth,	Saunders, Thomas, M.,	Jany.	8, 1767
Tart, Nathan,	Sanders, Sarah,	May	7, 1747
Nathan,	Hall, Priscilla,	Dec.	3, 1758
Nathan,	Garden, Elizabeth,	Mch.	31, 1771
Mary,	Chovin, Alexander,	Nov.	12, 1772
Sarah Amelia,	Bampfield, George,	Feb.	27, 1794
Thompson, Jane,	Green, William,	July	17, 1752
Thomson, Rebecca,	Johnston, Richard,	Mch.	23, 1761
Threadcraft, Mary,	Baker, Michael,	Sep.	7, 1727
Thomas,	Morrena, Magd'n,	July	15, 1745
Tiencken, John,	Poyas, Louisa Ann,	May	21, 1873

Townsend, William, Bedon, Sarah, Mch. 14, 1750
Tookerman, Richard, Warnock, Elizabeth, May 6, 1756
Tresvan, Theodorus, Scriven, Martha, Mrs., Feb. 24, 1720-1
Tresvin, William, Daniel, ——, Mrs., July 17, 1734
Trapier, Paul, Horrey, Magdalen, Sep. 22, 1743
Turkitt, Sarah, Bellin, James, Sep. 19, 1713
    Mary, Ford, Joseph, Mch. 5, 1716-7
Tyran, Anna, Clerk, Joseph, Mch. 25, 1725

V.

Vanderhorst, John, Pollock, Marg't, Mrs., Sep. 8, 1714
    Arnoldus, Simons, Elizabeth, July 18, 1745
    Joseph, Follingsby, Jane, May 14, 1758
Vanal, Elizabeth, Leroux, John, June 26, 1757
    Hester, Ellis, Samuel, Aug. 12, 1770
Verine, Jean, Mrs., Plumer, Moses, Feb. 15, 1712-3
Vicaridge, John, Ashby, Elizabeth, Mch. —, 17—

W.

Waties, Thomas, Alston, Anne, Sep. 1, 1751
Watts, Thomas, Taylor, Susannah, Oct. 12, 1756
Warnock, Mary, Roper, Jeremiah, Dec. 8, 1711
    Mary, Darby, Michael, May 21, 1751
    Samuel, Hartley, Magdalen
        Elizabeth, June 12, 1755
    Elizabeth, Tookerman, Richard, May 6, 1756
    Anna, Bennet, Thomas, June 9, 1774
Warbeuf, Hannah, Poole, William, Dec. 8, 1726
Wallbank, Hannah, Goodbie, John, Dec. 29, 1713
    Ruth, Bonny, Thomas, Sep. 14, 1721
Walker, Martha, Cart, Joseph, Dec. 14, 1760
    Ann, Boyd, Robert, Sep. 19, 1762
    Elizabeth, Martin, Edward, Jany. 20, 1763
Ward, J. M., Sanders, Mary, Mrs., Sep. 5, 1859
    John, Elfe, Emily W., Mch. 21, 1871
Wells, Edger, Roper, Lidia, June 29, 1709

Wells, William,	Dubois, Frances,	Oct.	20, 1774
Welsh, George,	Ettering, Margaret,	Aug.	6, 1767
White, Mary,	Davis, Joseph,	July	10, 1754
John,	Roddam, Sarah,	Aug.	6, 1774
Marianne			
Susannah,	Hood, Jesse,	Dec.	28, 1855
Whitesides, Sarah,	Arthur, George,	Oct.	30, 1772
Whilden, Jonathan,	King, Ann,	Dec.	19, 1749
John,	Murrell, Susannah,	Feb.	20, 1755
Withers, Richard,	Paris, Elizabeth,	Apl.	10, 1755
William,	Hartley, Rebecca,	Nov.	27, 1755
Thomas,	Deveaux, Mary Carl'e,	Apl.	8, 1778
Witten, Thomas,	Stanley, Elizabeth,	Aug.	15, 1718
Wigfall, Sarah,	Hasell, Andrew,	Mch.	28, 1751
Joseph,	Durand, Susannah,	Nov.	3, 1768
Benjamin,	Dutarque, Martha,	Aug.	1, 1771
Williams, Leah,	Martin, William,	Nov.	25, 1777
Wood, Susannah,	Basselleu, Louis,	Aug.	27, 1775
Wright, William,	Howard, Sarah,	Mch.	19, 1711–2

Y.

Young, Archibald,	Simons, Martha,	Nov.	22, 1726
Benjamin,	Alston, Martha,	June	7, 1761

When they shall rise from the dead, they neither marry, nor are given in marriage; but are as the angels which are in heaven. St. Mark, xii, 25.

REGISTER

OF

BIRTHS AND BAPTISMS.

BIRTHS AND BAPTISMS.

Baptism doth also now save us. 1 St. Peter, iii., 21.

A.

Addison—Parents—Thomas and Mary.
        Joseph . . . . bap. May 10, 1771
        Martha . . . . bap. Oct. 22, 1774
Aiken, 1—Parents—James and Sarah.
        Elizabeth . . . . born Sept. 24, 1742
        James . . . . born Mch. 15, 1743
        Mary. . . . . born Oct. 6, 1745
        Thomas . . . . born Nov. 3, 1747
    2—Parents—Thomas and Ann.
        Thomas . . . . bap. May 6, 1777
Alston—Parents—Peter and Sarah.
        Sarah Margaret . . . . bap. Dec. 18, 1748
Anderson—Parents—David and Mary Judon.
        Mary. . . . . bap. Jan'y 22, 1758
        David . . . . bap. Feb. 28, 1762
        John . . . . born July 1, 1764
        Daniel . . . . bap. June 12, 1768
        Martha . . . . bap. June 30, 1771
        Philip . . . . bap. April 2, 1775
        John . . aged 55 years . bap. July 24, 1768
Ashby, 1—Parents—John and Constantia.
        John . . . . { born Mch. 16, 1697-8
                         { bap. Mch. 24, ——
        Thomas, ... born Jan. 25, ——

Ashby, 2—Parents—Thomas and Elizabeth LeJeau.

Thomas . . . . . . { born Jan. 25, 1721-2 / bap. Feb. 22, ———

Elizabeth . . . . . { born Nov. 2, 1723 / bap. Dec. 23, ———

Constantia. . . . . { born Jan. 10, 1725·6 / bap. Feb. 19, ———

3—Parents—Thos. and Marg't Hen'ta Bonneau.

Thomas. . . . . bap, Apl. 5, 1752
Anthony . . . . bap. Apl. 21, 1754
Mary. . . . . bap. June 13, 1756

4—Parents—John and Mary Bonneau.

John . . . . bap. Feb. 1, 1759

5—Parents—Thomas and Anne Peyre.

Hannah . . . . . . { born Nov. 28, 1774 / bap. Jan. 13, 1775
Margaret Mary . . . . bap. June 24, 1776
Anne . . . . bap. Jan. 16, 1778
Elizabeth. . . . . . born Feb. 17, 1779
Thomas . . . . born Dec. 21, 1783

Auger—Parents—Nicholas and Hannah.

Mary . . . . { born May 5, 1712–3 / bap. June —, ———

Axson—Parents—William and Eliz'th Susn'h Mouzon.

Elizabeth . . . . . . { born Dec. 12, 1762 / bap. Feb. 27, 1763

Jehu } twins . . . · { born Nov. 29, 1764
John } { bap. Apl. 14, 1765

B.

Ball, 1—Parents—Thomas and Frances.

Richard . . . . . . { born Dec. 3, 1711 / bap. June 29, 1712
Thomas . . . . born Nov. 25, 1713

2—Parents—John Cuming and ———.

John Cuming . . . . . born Apl. 17, 1748

3—Parents—John and ———·

Eleanor . . . . bap. June 12, 1763

Ball, 4—Parents—William J., Jr., and Catherine T. Gibbs.

William James . . . . bap. Mch. 30, 1870

Isaac Gibbs . . . . . .   Apl. 21, 1872

Catharine . . . . . . $\begin{cases} \text{born Jan. 7, 1874} \\ \text{bap. Apl. 20, ——} \end{cases}$

5—Parents—John and Edith Prioleau.

John . . . . bap. Apl. 16, 1871

Bailey—Parents—Roberts S. and Eliza L., of Mt. Pleasant.

Edward. . . . . . . $\begin{cases} \text{born May 23, 1843} \\ \text{bap. July 30, ——} \end{cases}$

Baker, 1—Parents—Ebenezer and Hannah.

Henry . . . . born Jan. 2, 1702–3

Michael . . . . born Sep. 19, 1706

2—Parents—Michael and Mary.

Elizabeth . . . . . . born Oct. 29, 1727

Beech—Parents—Christopher and Mary.

Richard . . . . . . born Jan. 11, 1694–5

Grace Mary . . . . born July 11, 1696

Mary . . . . born Sep. 18, 1698

Christopher . . . . . born Aug. 5, 1700

Grace . . . . born Nov. 7, 1702

Christiana . . . . . born Sep. 24, 1704

John . . . . born Sep. 6, 1706

Joseph . . . . born Sep. 2, 1708

Martha . . . . . . born July 27, 1710

Beresford, 1—Parents—Richard, Esq., and Sarah Cooke.

John . . . . $\begin{cases} \text{born Nov. 18, 1712} \\ \text{bap. Nov. 27, ——} \end{cases}$

2—Parents—Richard, Esq.,and Dorothy Mellish.

Richard . . . . . . born Jan. 31, 1719–20

3—Parents—Richard and Sarah Logan.

Richard . . . . bap. June 3, 1755

Sarah . .   . . bap. Jan. 8, 1758

Bellin—Parents—James and Sarah Turkitt.

William . . . . born Apl. 23, 1715

Sarah . . . . born Sep. 1?, 1717

Allard . . . . born Nov. 6, 1719

James . . . . born Sep. 16, 1722

Mary . . . . born Feb. 1, 1724–5

4

Besselleu—Parents—Philip and Susannah.

Mark Anthony . . . $\begin{cases} \text{born Oct. 22, 1774} \\ \text{bap. Nov. 13, ———} \end{cases}$

Charles . . . . . . $\begin{cases} \text{born May 14, 1776} \\ \text{bap. July 21, ———} \end{cases}$

Philip Anthony . . . $\begin{cases} \text{born Feb. 27, 1778} \\ \text{bap. Mch. 17, ———} \end{cases}$

Lewis . . . . $\begin{cases} \text{born Mch. 26, 1779} \\ \text{bap. Apl. 6, ———} \end{cases}$

Bernard—Parents—Benjamin John, of Santee, and Ann.

Benjamin . . . . bap. Jan. 21, 1776

Bird—Parents—John Thomas and Anne Rivers.

John . . . . born Dec. 17, 1754

Blundell—Parents—Samuel and Anna.

John . . . . born Aug. 17, 1701

Thomas . . . .   Dec. 23, 1704

Bossard—Parents—Henry and Elizabeth.

Elizabeth. . . . . . . born Jan. 28, 1720–1

John, Susannah, } twins . . $\begin{cases} \text{born Mch. 20, 1722–3} \\ \text{bap. May 15, ———} \end{cases}$

Anna Judith . . . . born Dec. 19, 1725

Henry . . . . born Feb. 19, 1730

Bonny—Parents—Thomas and Ruth.

Anna . . . . born June 24, 1721

Bonneau, 1—Parents—Anthony, Jr., and ———

——— . . . . born July 23, 1732

Anthony . . . . bap. Sep. 23, 1743

2—Parents—Peter and Hester.

Magdalen . . . . born Mch. 29, 1738

Hester . . . . born May 12, 1740

Peter . . . . born Aug. 12, 1744

Anthony . . . . ——— ——— ———

3—Parents—Elias and Susannah Miller.

Elias   . . . . born Nov. 23, 17—

Susannah . . . . born Apl. 18, 1741

Elias . . . . born July 10, 1743

Mary . . . . born July 20, 1745

Judith . . . . born July 30, 1747

Stephen . . . . born Jan. 4, 1748-9

Bonneau, 3—Parents—Elias and Susannah Miller.

Anne . . . . born Jan. 18, 1750

Michael . . . . born Nov. 23, 1752

Elisha . . . . born Feb. 4, 1755

4—Parents—Elias and Mary.

Magdalene . . . . born May 18, 1757

Mary . . . . bap. July 12, 1761

Borland—Parents—William and Mary.

William . . . . born May 27, 1724

Bochett, 1—Parents—Henry and Ann Jennens.

Anne . . . . born Aug. 15, 1747

Henry . . . . born Aug. 11, 1749

Nicholas } twins . . . { born Jan. 22, 1753
Mary, } { bap. Apl. 1, ——

Frances . . . . bap. Apl. 20, 1755

2—Parents—Peter and Frances Dubois.

Peter . . . . born Oct. 18, 1755

Hester . . . . born Jan. 8, 1758

3—Parents—Anthony and Hester Mouzon.

Anthony . . . . born Oct. 29, 1757

4—Parents—Lewis and Mary Ashby.

Lewis . . . . born Apl. 27, 1766

Anthony . . . . { born May 28, 1768
{ bap. July 24, ——

Margarett Henrietta . . . born Jan. 5, 1772

Bonoist—Parents—John and Mary.

Samuel . . . . { born Aug. 5, 1751
{ bap. Feb. 19, 1753

Bourke—Parents—Armsby and Mary—in Charleston.

Isabella . . . . { born June 23, 1847
{ bap. July 1, in ex.

Boddom—Parents—Joseph and Mary.

Mary Priscilla . . . . { born Mch.—, 1791
{ bap. May 29, ——

Boucher—Parents—William and Mary.

William . . . . born Oct. 15, 1732

Brockinton—Parents—William and Sarah Griffin.

Sarah . . . . born Aug. 6, 1716

Mary . . . . born Nov. 6, 1719

Elizabeth . . . . born Aug. 15, 1721

Bremar, 1—Parents—Peter and Elizabeth Shekelford.

Francis . . . . brn. Feb.9,1719-20

Elizabeth Sarah . . . . . brn. Jan.22, 1725-6

Sarah . . . . { born July 10, 1725 / bap. Aug. 16, ——

2—Parents—John and Vollentine Shekelford.

Mary . . . . { born Feb. 27, 1730 / bap. May, 30, ——

3—Parents—Francis and Martha.

Hester . . . . born Sep. 15, 1745

Brindley—Parents—John George and Mary.

Mary } twins . . . . . { bap. Jan. 22, 1769
Anne }

Sarah . . . . bap. Feb. 18, 1770

Helen . . . . bap. Nov. 15, 1771

Hester . . . . bap. Apl. 2, 1775

Mary—an adult . . . . . bap. Mch. 20, 1768

Burdell—Parents—Jacob and Elizabeth Carriere.

Elizabeth . . . . born Feb. 4, 1715-6

William . . . . born Oct. 4, 1717

Burton—Parents—Thomas and Mary.

Sarah . . . . born Feb.19,1707-8

Mary . . . . born Apl 19, 1710

Thomas . . . . born Nov. 28, 1718

Burdeaux—Parents—Israel and ——

Israel . . . . —— —— ——

Burnham—Parents—Benjamin and Anne.

Charles . . . . bap. Nov. 25, 1745

Butler—Parents—Thomas and Mary.

Thomas . . . . bap. Aug. 9, 1772

—————— . . . . bap. Sept. 20, 1774

Bullock—Parents—Samuel and Rhoda Hales.

Giles . . . . { born Feb. 27, 1776 / bap. Nov. 21, ——

C

Carriere—Parents—John and Elizabeth.

John . . . . { born Nov. 18, 1712 / bap. Dec. 28, ——

Cart—Parents—Joseph and Martha Walker.

John . . . . bap. Apl. 26, 1763

Cape—Parents—Brian and Mary Hetherington.

Brian . . . . $\begin{cases} \text{born Feb. 15, 1775} \\ \text{bap. Nov. 16, ——} \end{cases}$

Carrol—Parents—Mordecai and Rachel.

Elizabeth . . . . bap. July 13, 1771
Sarah . . . . bap. July 13, 1771
Edward . . . . bap. July 13, 1771

Cahusac—Parents—Peter and Mary.

Ann . . . . bap. Dec. 26, 1763

Chevers—Parents—Philip and Elizabeth.

Hannah . . . . born Jan. 17, 1704-5
Anna . . . . born May 28, 1710
Sarah . . . . born June 8, 1712

Chambers—Parents—Thomas and Margaret.

Joseph . . . . $\begin{cases} \text{born June 26, 1723} \\ \text{bap. Oct. 11, ——} \end{cases}$

Chovin—Parents—Alexander and Hester.

Isaac . . . . bap. July 5, 1745

Clyatt—Parents—Robert and Hannah Stone.

Samuel . . . . born June 29, 1714
Samuel . . . . born Nov. 13, 1716
David . . . . born June 21, 1718
Stephen . . . . born Apl. 28, 1722

Conyers—Parents—John and Mary Quarterman.

James . . . . born May 24, 1718
Elizabeth Honor . . . . born Feb. 27, 1720-1

Commander—Parents—Samuel and Elizabeth.

Samuel . . . . born Jan. 22, 1705-6
John . . . . born Ap'l 6, 1708
Hannah . . . . born Jan. 10, 1709-10
Joseph . . . . born Aug. 1, 1712

Codner—Parents—Richard and Selina.

Charles Burnham . . . $\begin{cases} \text{born Dec. 11, 1710} \\ \text{bap. Dec. 26, 1712} \end{cases}$
Margaret . . . . born June 26, 1713
Phœbe . . . . born Dec. 27, 1716
———— son . . . . . . born June 9, 1719

Codner, 2.—Parents—Charles and Ann.

Richard . . . . . . { born Aug. 19, 1732 / bap. 1733

Charles . . . . born Ap'l 14, 1734

Sabina . . . . { born Nov. 26, 1735 / bap. May 8, 1736

Collings—Parents—Jonathan and Mary Ann Simons.

Mary Ann . . . . . . born Feb. 5, 1744

Jonathan . . . . born Mch 25, 1748

Cooke—Parents—Edward and Mary Burnham.

Sarah . . . . bap. Ap'l 26, 1761

Combe—Parents—John and Jane.

Mary Sarah . . . . . bap. Jan. 27, 1764

Cox—Parents—John and Mary.

Francis Alex . . . . { born Dec. —, 1828 / bap. Jan. 5, 1829

2.—Parents—John and Elizabeth.

John Howell . . . . { born Mch 12, 1831 / bap. May 1, ——

3.—Parents—Thomas C. and Sarah Anderson.

Charles Wesley, 3 years . bap. Sept. 8, 1867

Walter Sessions . . . . bap. Sept. 8, 1867

4.—Parents—George W. and ———.

Robert Muirhead . . . . bap. Feb. 3, 1867

Coward—Parents—Wilson and Feronia.

Martha Eliza . . . . . bap. May 11, 1856

Cuming—Parents—John and Naomi

Hester . . . . bap. July 31, 1748

Benjamin . . . . . . born Jan. 7, 1744

Cummins—Parents—John and Ann.

—— son . . . . . . born Oct. 6, 1765

Cusack—Parents—Adam and Frances Oran.

—— son . . . . . . born July —, 1765

—— d. . . . . born Dec. —, 1767

D.

Daniel—Parents—Robert and Martha.

Sarah . . . . born Nov. 6, 1703
Martha . . . . born Dec. 29, 1704
John . . . . born Mch 29, 1707
Anna . . . . born Ap'l 15, 1710

2.—Parents—Marmaduke and Susan.

Marmaduke . . . . . born Dec. 13, 1725
Sarah Procter . . . . . born Jan. 17, 1727-8

2.—Parents—Robert and Elizabeth Russ.

Robert ⎫ twins . . . born Feb. 17, 1756
Jonathan ⎭

Martha . . . . ⎰ born Feb. 28, 1758
⎱ bap. Ap'l 6, ——

Sarah . . . . bap. May 4, 1760

Elizabeth . . . . . . ⎰ born Mch 15, 1763
⎱ bap. June 7, ——

Robert Litton . . . . ⎰ born May 24, 1764
⎱ bap. July 18, ——

Martha . . . . bap. Jan. 23, 1766

Elizabeth Russ . . . ⎰ born Mch 18, 1766
⎱ bap. June 7, ——

Martha . . . . bap. Ap'l 11, 1768

Dawson—Parents—Richard and Margaret.

Richard . . . . born June 22, 1709
Sarah . . . . born June 4, 1714

Darby—Parents—Michael and Mary Warnock.

Hannah . . . . born Sept. 21, 1718
Joseph . . . . born Dec. 8, 1722
Mary . . . . born Nov. 15, 1725

2.—Parents—Michael and Elizabeth.

——d . . . . . . born Jan. 9, 1732-3

3.—Parents—Michael and Judith.

Judith . . . . ⎰ born Nov. 20, 1734
⎱ bap. Aug. —, ——

4.—Parents—Michael and Susannah.

Michael Videau . . . ⎰ born Ap'l 9, 1739
⎱ bap. May 8, ——

Danzy—Parents—Richard and Sarah Crouch.

William . . . . . . $\begin{cases} \text{born Nov. 25, 1724} \\ \text{bap. Jan. 3, 1725} \end{cases}$

Davis, 1—Parents—Isaac and Deborah.

Daniel . . . . born Feb. 11, 1717–8

Joseph . . . . born Nov. 9, 1719

Mary . . . . born Nov. 14; 1725

2—Parents—Andrew and Ann.

David . . . . bap. Aug. 4, 1775

Mary . . . . bap. Aug. 4, 1775

Ann . . . . bap. Aug. 4, 1775

Dehay—Parents—John Andrew and Margaret.

John . . . . $\begin{cases} \text{born Oct. 14, 1731} \\ \text{bap. Nov. —, ——} \end{cases}$

Sarah . . . . born July 15, 1737

Dearington, 1—Parents—Thomas and Patience.

John . . . . born Apl. 21, 1745

Richard . . . . . . bap. Oct. 18, 1747

2—Parents—Robert and Ann.

Mary . . . . born Jan. 12, 1778

Deveaux—Parents—Andrew and Mary.

Andrew . . . . bap. June 18, 1765

John . . . . bap. July 15, 1767

Donnelly—Parents—Edward and Margaret.

Elinor . . . . born June 7, 1718

Mary . . . . born Aug. 5, 1721

Edward . . . . born Jan. 3, 1726–7

Margaret . . . . . . born Jan. 20, 1728

Ann . . . . born Oct. 1, 1731

Elizabeth . . . . . . born Sep. 7, 1736

Elizabeth . . . . . . born Sep. 9, 1737

Doorne—Parents—William and ——

Sarah . . . . bap. Aug. 26, 1768

Droes—Parents—Isaac and Jean.

Daniel . . . . born Oct. 13, 1723

Isaac . . . . born Oct. 26, 1725

Drake—Parents—Edward and Anne Ruberry.

Edward . . . . bap. Apl. 4, 1756

DuPre, 1—Parents—Cornelius and Jean Brabant.

Jean Elizabeth . . . . { born Oct. 12, 1709 / bap. Nov. 13, ——

Mary Magdalen . . . { born Nov. 15, 1711 / bap. Nov. 26, ——

2—Parents—Josias and Sarah.

Josias Garnier . . . . born Sep. 17, 1705

Elizabeth . . . . born Oct. 3, 1710

Sarah . . . . born Nov. 1, 1713

Sarah . . . . born Dec. 13, 1716

Samuel Gobbaille . . . born July 7, 1718

3—Parents—Josias and Ann.

Ann . . . . born July 30, 1728

4—Parents—Josias and Anne.

Anne . . . . bap. Apl. 14, 1754

Elizabeth . . . . bap. June 15, 1755

Josias Blake . . . . . . bap. Dec. 25, 1756

Dutarque, 1—Parents—Lewis and Christian Maria.

Esther . . . . born July 10, 1704

John . . . . born June 19, 1707

Anna . . . . born Mch. 24, 1710

Mary . . . . born Sep. 8, 1712

Sarah . . . . born Dec. 9, 1719

Mary . . . . born Aug. 11, 1722

Joseph . . . . born Oct. 13, 1724

2—Parents—John and Mary.

John . . . . { born June 1, 1734 / bap. July —, ——

Noah . . . . born Sep. 6, 1735

Christian . . . . born Jan. 7, 1738

Catharine . . . . born Jan. 7, 173–

Mary . . . . born June 15, 1741

Lewis . . . . bap. Dec. 29, 1744

Sarah . . . . bap. July 5, 1747

Martha . . . . bap. Mch. 9, 1752

Catharine . . . . bap. Feb. 15, 1760

3—Parents—John, Jr., and Mary Serre.

Judith . . . . bap. Jan. 17, 1766

Dutart—Parents—Charles John and Mary E.

Samuel Wm. . . . . . . { born Sep. 30, 1838
{ bap. Mch. 1, 1843

Jane Catharine . . . . { born Mch. 13, 1840
{ bap. Mch. 1, 1843

Ann Eliza . . . . . { born Aug. 5, 1841
{ bap. Mch. 1, 1841

Emma Julia . . . . . { born June 12, 1842
{ bap. May 6, 1845

Martha Harriet . . . { born Nov. 10, 1843
{ bap. May 6, 1845

Charles John . . . . { born Feb 11, 1846
{ bap. May 14, 1846

Durant—Parents—Henry and Ann.

Hannah . . . . born Nov. 15, 1712
Anna . . . . born Sep. 18, 1718
John . . . . born Aug. 27, 1721
Henry . . . . born Dec. 26, 1724
George . . . . born —— — 1730

Dunham—Parents—John and Hannah.

John . . . . born May 26, 1714
Hannah . . . . born June 7, 1717
Sarah . . . . born Jan. 29, 1720–1

Durfey—Parents—Hugh and Austins.

Thomas . . . . bap. June 17, 1744
Hugh . . . . born Mch. 7, 1746

Dutton—Parents— —— and ——

Mary . . . . bap. June 17, 1744

Dubois, 1—Parents—John and Sarah Mouzon.

Judith . . . . bap. Mch. 15, 1761

2—Parents—Peter and Ann Mouzon.

Ann,
Elizabeth, } twins . . . . bap. Apl. 11, 1764

Judith . . . . bap. Feb. 8, 1767
Peter . . . . bap. Feb. 27, 1774
Caroline . . . . . . bap. Jan. 1, 1778

Robert Quash,
Mary Ann } twins . bap. Oct. —, 1769

Dubois, 3—Parents—James and Hester Guerin.

Hester . . . . bap. June 29, 1765
Susannah . . . . bap. July 8, 1766
Frances . . . . bap. Mch. 1, 1769
Elizabeth Paget . . . . bap. July 13, 1771

E

Edwards, 1—Parents—Peter and Patience.

Mary . . . . born Mch. 5, 1712–3

2—Parents—Edward and Mary.

Anna . . . . born May 9, 1725
Newell . . . . born Mch. 16, 1727-8
Edward . . . . { born Mch. 31, 1730 / bap. May 9, ——
Robert . . . . born Nov. 26, 1734

3—Parents—Dr. Charles and ——

Susan Elizabeth . . . { born — —, 1828 / bap. Apl. 12, 1829
Francis Marion . . . { born Feb. 24, 1831 / bap. May 8, ——
Catharine . . . . bap. Apl. 20, 1834

4—Parents—Daniel C., and ——

Maria Antonia . . . . { born Mch. 24, 1832 / bap. May 5, 1833

Elliot, 1—Parents—William and ——

Thomas . . . . bap. June 17, 1744

2—Parents—John and Mary Bullock.

John Childs . . . . . { born Jan. 14, 1758 / bap. July 5, ——

Ellis—Parents—Samuel and Hester Vanal.

Elizabeth . . . . bap. Ap'l 28, 1775
Elizabeth . . . . . . bap. July 15, 1777

Elfe—Parents—George and Eliza J.

Emily Hayne . . . . { born Sept. 9, 1842 / bap. Ap'l 14, 1843
Robert Edward . . . { born Jan. 23, 1844 / bap. May 5, ——
William W. C. . . . . { born Sept. 12, 1845 / bap. Feb. 1, 1850
George Edwards . . . { born Ap'l 9, 1847 / bap. Feb. 1, 1850

Elfe—Parents—George and Eliza J.

William Simmons . . { born Feb. 7, 1849 / bap. Feb. 1, 1850

Anna Sarah . . . . . { born Feb. 14, 1851 / bap. May 6, 1855

Martha Ann . . . . { born Feb. 1, 1853 / bap. May 6, 1855

Clement Augustus . . { born Feb. 23, 1855 / bap. May 6, 1855

Eliza Slann . . . . . { born Dec. 8, 1856 / bap. Ap'l 25, 1857

Susan Caroline . . . { born Oct. 14, 1858 / bap. May 3, 1859

F.

Farrar—Parents—Benjamin and Mary.

Mary . . . . bap. May 28, 1765

Finlayson—Parents—Mungo and Mary Ann Hartley.

Mungo Graeme . . . . bap. Aug. 25, 1776

Ford—Parents—Nathaniel and Mary Beresford King.

John . . . . born Nov. 28, 1714

William . . . . born Mch. 10, 1722–3

2.—Parents— ——— and ———

Fred'rck August's, adult...bap. Dec. 6, 1829

Ffoord—Parents—Ebenezer and Judith.

Sarah . . . . born Apl. 16, 1725

Joseph . . . . born Nov. 21, 1727

Fogartie, 1—Parents—John and Mary.

Stephen . . . . born Nov. 22, 1698

Lidia . . . . born Aug. 28, 1702

John . . . . born Dec. 13, 1704

Edmond . . . . born Ap'l 8, 1708

Mary . . . . born Sept. 7, 1709

Hannah . . . . born Mch 31, 1713

James . . . . born June 2, 1715

Patience . . . . born July 2, 1717

Sarah . . . . born June 6, 1719

David . . . . born July 10, 1722

Fogartie, 2.—Parents—Stephen and Esther Dutarque.
Stephen . . . . born Feb. 26, 1721–2
Joseph . . . . born Jan. 26, 1723–4
Lewis Dutarque . . . . born May 1, 1726
3.—Parents—James and Margaret Amelia Garden.
Esther . . . . born ——— ———
Joseph . . . . born Aug. 17, 1782
4.—Parents Stephen D. and Amanda.
Stephen Arthur . . . . bap. Sept. 1, 1855
Irving . . . . bap. Ap'l 26, 1862
Louisa Poyas, 4 years . bap. Aug. 13, 1870
Amanda Rembert, 4 m's.bap. Aug. 13, 1870
5.—Parents—— and Mrs. S. A. (widow) Charleston.
Marion . . . . • . . bap. May 1, 1874
Frewin—Parents—Charles and Ann Simons.
Francis Charles . . . . born Ap'l 9, 1768
Frasier—Parents—John and Mary Duke,
John . . . . bap. Nov. 24, 1774
Freeman—Parents—John T. and Ella Dutart.
James Hamlin . . . . bap. Mch 11, 1877
Furman—Parents—Wood and Rachel.
Josiah . . . . born May 13, 1744
Sarah . . . . born May 6, 1752
Richard . . . . born Oct. 9, 1755

G.

Garden—Parents—Rev. Alexander and Amey Hartley.
John . . . . born Oct. 31, 1751
Elizabeth . . . . . . born Jan. 30, 1755
Margaret Amelia . . . . born Jan. 16, 1760
Alexander . . . . . . born Aug. 19, 1762
Gibson—Parents—Robert and Jane.
Anne . . . . { born July 24, 1769
{ bap. Sept. 28, ———
Goodbie—Parents—John and Hannah Wallbank.
Elizabeth . . . . born Oct. 1, 1714
John Wallbank . . . . born Dec. 24, 1720

Goddard—Parents—Capt. Francis and Mary Manwaring.

Mary . . . . born Feb. 28, 1717-8

Jenny . . . . born July 19, 1720

Frances . . . . { born June 20, 1724 / bap. Sep. 15, ——

Francis . . . . { born Feb. 26, 1725 / bap. July 17, ——

William . . . . . . { born Nov. 1, 1728 / bap. Dec. 25, ——

Goodmunduke—Parents—Thomas and Susannah.

Thomas . . . . born Apl. 13, 1735

Elizabeth . . . . born Jan. 26, 1736-7

Benjamin Duke . . . . . born Mch. 29, 1739

Susannah . . . . born Dec. 18, 1741

Mary . . . . born June 9, 1744

Greenwell—Parents—Zacharias and Mary.

Elias . . . . bap. Dec. 22, 1776

Gray—Parents—Henry and Ann.

Henry . . . . bap. Apl. 23, 1749

Anne . . . . bap. —— ——

Margaret, ... bap. Apl. 2, 1751

Peter . . . . bap. Apl. 25, 1753

Frances . . . ' . . . . bap. June 22, 1755

Mary . . . . bap. Feb. 27, 1757

Frances . . . . bap. Feb, 28, 1760

Guillard—Parents—Charles G., and Nancy, of St. James, Santee.

Theodore—7 mos. . . . bap. May 8, 1791

Guerin, 1—Parents—Vincent and Judith Guerin.

Isaac . . . . born Apl. 10, 1704

Susannah Elizabeth . . . born Sep. 18, 1706

John . . . . born Feb. 25, 1709-10

Judith . . . . born Feb. 20, 1711-2

Marian . . . . born Aug. 7, 1714

Peter . . . . born Mch. 27, 1717

Andrew . . . . born Dec. 13, 1720

Guerin, 2—Parents—Isaac and Martha Mouzon.

Isaac . . . . $\begin{cases} \text{born Mch. 5, 1731} \\ \text{bap. Apl. ——} \end{cases}$

Lewis . . . . $\begin{cases} \text{born Mch. 5, 1733} \\ \text{bap. May ——} \end{cases}$

Henry . . . . $\begin{cases} \text{born Mch. 14, 1736} \\ \text{bap. Apl. 18, ——} \end{cases}$

Robert . . . . $\begin{cases} \text{born June 21, 1738} \\ \text{bap. Aug. 7, ——} \end{cases}$

3—Parents—John and Elizabeth.
Vincent . . . . bap. Jan. 15, 1744
Elizabeth . . . . bap. Feb. 28, 1744
Mary Johnston . . . . . bap. Aug. 19, 1753
Robert . . . . bap. May 19, 1756

4—Parents—Robert and Sarah Sanders.
Martha Esther . . . . . bap. Feb. 8, 1761
Sarah . . . . . . bap. Sep. 11, 1763

5—Parents—Peter and Mary Ann Norman.
Martha . . . . bap. Nov. 24, 1751
Peter . . . . bap. Apl. 18, 1756
Susannah Isabella . . . bap. Sep. 20, 1761

6—Parents—Peter and Margaret.
James Bilbeau . . . . . bap. Oct. 28, 1764

7—Parents—Henry and Magdalene Bonneau.
Hester . . . . bap. Jan. 24, 1762
Isaac . . . . bap. Aug. 19, 1764

Henry . . . . $\begin{cases} \text{born Jan. 24, 1767} \\ \text{bap. May 10, ——} \end{cases}$

8—Parents—Vincent and Hester Dubois.
Videau . . . . bap. July 31, 1774
Elizabeth . . . . bap. May 29, 1776

9—Parents—Samuel and Frances Bochett.
—da . . . . bap. Apl. 16, 1775
George Gabriel . . . . . bap. Apl. 21, 1777

H

Hayes, 1—Parents—Charles and Sarah.

Charles . . . . born Aug. 28, 1710

Mary . . . . born Dec. 17, 1714

George . . . . born Jan. 16, 1718-19

Sarah . . . . born Jan. 25, 1721

2—Parents—Charles and Elizabeth Goodbie.

John . . . . born Nov. 9, 1731

Hamilton, 1—Parents—Archibald and Bridget Roche.

James . . . . born Sep. 2, 1727

2—Parents—William and Sarah.

John . . . . bap. Apl. 26, 1752

Mary . . . . bap. Apl. 26, 1752

Hall, 1—Parents—Thomas and Katharine.

Thomas . . . . bap. Mch. 20, 1747

2—Parents—John D. and Mary S.

George Abbott . . . { born April 2, 1844 / bap. Dec. 26, ——

John . . . . { born Feb. 5, 1846 / bap. May 14, ——

Hasell, 1—Parents—Rev. Thomas and Elizabeth Ashby.

Thomas . . . . . . { born Aug. 18, 1718 / bap. Sep. 7, ——

Constantia . . . . . { born Apl. 1, 1721 / bap. Apl. 24, ——

John . . . . { born Feb. 20, 1723-4 / bap. Mch. 20, ——

Elizabeth . . . . . { born Jan. 14, 1725-6 / bap. Feb. 20, ——

Andrew . . . . . . { born Mch. 22, 1729 / bap. Apl. 29, ——

Ann . . . . { born July 19, 1732 / bap. Aug. 20, ——

Mary . . . . { born July 29, 1734 / bap. Oct. 20, ——

Ann . . . . { born Mch. 9, 1736-7 / bap. May 10, ——

Hasell, 2—Parents—Thomas and Alice Morrit.

Thomas . . . . bap. Mch. 31, 1745
Elizabeth . . . . . . bap. Aug. 10, 1746

3—Parents—John and Hannah Simons.

John . . . . born Nov. 4, 1750

4—Parents—Andrew and Sarah Wigfall.

Sarah . . . . born Jan. 18, 1752
Constantia . . . . . . born Feb. 26, 1754
Andrew . . . . born Oct. 1, 1755

Harleston, 1—Parents—John and ———

John . . . . bap. Mch. 19, 1744
Isaac Child . . . . . bap, Dec. 18, 1745
Elizabeth . . . . bap. Mch. 16, 1747
Anne . . . . bap. Apl. 22, 1752
Nicholas . . . . bap. Mch. 5, 1754
Hannah . . . . bap. June 19, 1755
Sarah . . . . bap. Mch. 10, 1759
Edward . . . . bap. July 1, 1761

2—Parents—John and Elizabeth.

Elizabeth Cecilia . . . { born Apl. 5, 1830 / bap. May 8, 1831

3—Parents—John M. and Eleanor E.

Mary Elizabeth . . . { born July 23, 1843 / bap. Jan. 8, 1844

Sarah Gaillard . . . . { born July 13, 1845 / bap. May 6, 1846

Eleanor Cordes . . . { born June 29, 1846 / bap. Apl. 28, 1847

Martha Selina . . . . { born Oct. 21, 1847 / bap. Dec. 18, 1848

Hales—Parents—William and Eleanor.

Daniel . . . . bap. Sep. 1, 1768

Hamlin, 1—Parents—Samuel William and Sarah E.

George McDowell, . . { born Sep. 5, 1830 / bap. Apl. 11, 1831

William Henry . . . . { born Jan. 4, 1832 / bap. Oct. 24, 1833

Philipine Behn . . . . { born Aug.—, 1836 / bap. Feb. 14, 1837

5

Hamlin, 1—Parents—Samuel William and Sarah E.

Thomas Theodore . { born July 13, 1842 / bap. Apl. 18, 1844

2—Parents— —·—– and Widow A.

Roseanna—3 years . . . bap. Feb. 11, 1868

3—Parents—Thomas Theodore and Sallie.

Edward Swinton . . . . bap. July 15, 1877

Hanckel—Parents—Rev. J. Stuart and F. E.

John Elias Moore . . . bap. May 5, 1860

Hearty—Parents—David and Kezia.

Elijah . . . . born Nov. 15, 1729

Joel . . . . born Jan. 13, 1731

Herren—Parents—Zachariah and Margaret Manduvel.

Samuel . . . . bap. Mch. 21, 1776

How, 1—Parents—Robert and Susannah Elizabeth Guerin.

Robert . . . . { born Mch 12, 1729–30 / bap. May 10 ——

Elizabeth . . . . . . { born Sept. 19, 1731 / bap. Dec. ——

Thomas . . . . . . { born Dec. 9, 1732 / bap. Feb. 25, 1733

Judith . . . . { born May 6, 1734 / bap. May 17, ——

John . . . . { born Aug. 18, 1736 / bap. Sept. ——

Isaac . . . . { born Mch 2, 1737 / bap. Ap'l 30, ——

Mary . . . . { born Feb. 11, 1740 / bap. Feb. 20, ——

William . . . . born June 18, 1742

2—Parents—John and Susannah.

John . . . . bap. Oct. 5. 1777

Howard, 1—Parents—Thomas and Mary.

Experience . . . . . . born June 4, 1700

John . . . . born Feb. 14, 1704–5

Thomas . . . . born June 14, 1705

2—Parents—Edward and Letties Jones.

Edward . . . . born Sept. 4, 1717

Catharine . . . . . . born Mch 11, 1718–9

Howard, 2—Parents—Edward and Letties Jones.

Anna . . . . born Nov. 1, 1720
George . . . . born Jan. 9, 1723-4
Sarah . . . . born Ap'l 10, 1725
Elenor . . . . . . { born Dec. 22, 1728
{ bap. Mch 11, 1729

Huger, 1—Parents—Daniel and Anne Lejeau.

Francis . . . . bap. Aug. 1, 1751

2—Parents—Dr. Benjamin and Sarah.

Sarah Quash . . . . . bap. Ap'l 13, 1834

Hutson—Parents—Samuel J. and Melissa.

Melison Daisy . . . . . bap. Oct. 5, 1873

I.

I'On—Parents—Jacob and Mary.

Sarah Bond . . . . . . bap. May 14, 1778

I'Ons—Parents—Robert and Keziah.

Littlebury . . . . . . bap. May 6, 1770
William . . . . bap. May 6, 1770

J.

Jaudon, 1—Parents—Daniel and ——

Daniel . . . . born Jan. 19, 1709-10
Susannah Elizabeth . . born Ap'l 30, 1711
Noah . . . . born July 2, 1713
Elias . . . . born Aug. 21, 1715
Matthew . . . . . . born Sept. 23, 1717
Sarah . . . . born Feb. 24, 1719-20
Esther . . . . born June 27, 1722
Paul . . . . born Sept. 21, 1724

2—Parents—Paul and Martha Guerin.

Paul . . . . bap. May 25, 1773

3—Parents—Peter and ——

Sarah . . . . bap. Aug. 1, 1774

Jefferds, 1—Parents—John and Magdalen Miller.

John . . . . bap. June 5, 1753

Jeffords, 1—Parents—Daniel and Judith Bona.

——d . . . . born June 19, 1765

Jeffords, 1—Parents—Daniel and Judith Bona.

Daniel . . . . { born Aug. 27, 1766 / bap. Nov. 13, ——

John . . . . { born May 26, 1768 / bap. Sept. 3, ——

Daniel . . . . { born Dec. 3, 1771 / bap. Feb. 11, 1772

Elizabeth Judith . . . { born Jan. 9, 1774 / bap. Mch 22, ——

Margaret . . . . . . { born Ap'l 8, 1776 / bap. June 27, ——

Lewis . . . . { born Feb. 25, 1778 / bap. June 29, ——

Jenkins—Parents—Thomas and Mary Johnson.

Thomas . . . . born Dec. 30, 1719
Richard . . . . born Feb. 24, 1721-2

Jennens—Parents—James and Mary.

James . . . . born Aug. 20, 1718
Edward . . . . born Sept. 11, 1720
Thomas . . . . born Jan. 25, 1722-3

Jennings—Parents—James and Elizabeth.

Anne . . . . bap. Mch 5, 1754
James Jonathan . . . . bap. May 28, 1757

Johnson—Parents—Peter and Mahetabal.

Joseph . . . . born Nov. 15, 1699
Mary . . . . born Nov. 15, 1702
James . . . . born Aug. 14, 1794
Lidia . . . . born Nov. 30, 1705
Leah . . . . born Jan. 20, 1706-7

2—Parents—Peter and Deborah.

Peter . . . . { born Feb. 8, 1725-6 / bap. Apl. 17, ——

3—Parents—Robert and Sarah.

Robert . . . . born Apl. 18, 1733

Johnston, 1—Parents—Robert and Elizabeth Aiken.

Sarah . . . . bap. Mch. 9, 1760

2—Parents—Robert and Susannah.

Mary Brunit . . . . { born June 22, 1764 / bap. Sep. 16, ——

Johnston, 2—Parents—Robert and Susannah.

Priscilla . . . . . . { born Mch. 22, 1766 / bap. July 8, ——

Robert . . . . born Oct. 10, 1768

Sarah . . . . { born June 11, 1771 / bap. Jan. 12, 1772

Elizabeth . . . . . . { born Dec. 3, 1772 / bap. Apl. 25, 1773

Charles, } twins . . . { born Dec. 1, 1773
Susannah, } { bap. Mch. 13, 1774

Lydia . . . . bap. June 12, 1775

David . . . . { born July 4, 1776 / bap. Oct. 13, ——

John William . . . . { born Feb. 18, 1778 / bap. May 3, ——

Joly—Parents—John Gabriel and Esther.

Esther . . . . born Feb. 28, 1724-5

John . . . . born Nov. 25, 1725

James Thomas . . . . . born Mch. 28, 1727

Joel—Parents—Thomas and Hester Dutarque.

Thomas . . . . . . { born July 21, 1764 / bap. Oct. 1, ——

Mary . . . . { born Sept. 5, 1765 / bap. Sept. —— ——

——— . . . . bap. —— 1767

Jordan—Parents—James F. and Jane.

Alice Jane . . . . . { born Jan. 29, 1844 / bap. Jan. 17, 1846

Rose Eudora . . . . { born May 5, 1845 / bap. Jan. 17, 1846

June—Parents—John and Anna Howard.

John . . . . born Ap'l 18, 1721

Anna . . . . born Jan. 16, 1723-4

Peter . . . . born Ap'l 27, 1726

K.

Kayler—Parents—Richard and Mary.

Richard . . . . bap. Jan. 17, 1778

Ker—Parents—John and Jane.

Robert . . . . bap. Mch 13, 1774

Kennedy—Parents—Andrew J. and Martha R.

Hugh Reid . . . . . { born Mch 15, 1836 / bap. Ap'l 30, 1843

Joseph . . . . . . { born Aug. 20, 1839 / bap. Ap'l 30, 1843

King, 1—Parents—Samuel and Elizabeth Preston.

Elizabeth . . . . born July 21, 1707
Mary . . . . born Sept. 20, 1708
Anna . . . . born Aug. 23, 1710
Thomas . . . . born Mch 14, 1713–4
Samuel . . . . born Feb. 28, 1715–6
Sarah . . . . born Aug. 9, 1717
Martha . . . . born Dec. 11, 1719
Esther . . . . born Aug. 30, 1722
Anna . . . . born Jan. 27, 1724–5
George . . . . born Mch. 26, 1727
———— ———— . . . born July 26, 1732

2—Parents—Richard and Mary Beresford.

Charles . . . . born Feb. 15, 1709-10
Mary . . . . born Oct. 6, 1712

3—Parents—Robert and Hannah Marbeust.

Anna . . . . born June 12, 1716

4—Parents—Charles and Mary Johnson.

Mary Ann . . . . . . { born Aug. —, 1734 / bap. Sept. —, ——

Mary . . . . { born Oct. 19, 1737 / bap. Nov. —, ——

Richard . . . . . . { born Jan. 6, 1739 / bap. Feb. 12, ——

5—Parents—George and Catharine.

Samuel . . . . bap. Oct. 3, 1768

Knighten—Parents—Moses and Susannah.

Peter . . . . bap. Dec. 9, 1773

Koester—Parents—L. F. and ————

John Louis Frederick . . bap. July 24, 1870

L

Law—Parents—Joseph and Sarah Henly.

Hepsibah . . . . bap. Jan. 19, 1755

Laurens—Parents—Dr. Richard and Lucy.

Anna Isabella . . . . . bap. Apl. 23, 1854

Lesesne—Parents—Isaac, Sr. and Elizabeth.

Isaac . . . . born Sept. 5, 1709

Henry James . . . . . born Nov. 16, 1711

Esther . . . . born Jan. 28, 1714–5

Sarah . . . . born Sep. 4, 1716

Daniel . . . . born Jan. 29, 1718–9

2—Parents—Isaac 3d, and ———

Peter George . . . . { born Nov. 2, 1731 / bap. Feb. 20, 1732

3—Parents—Isaac, Jr., and Frances Netherton.

Francis . . . . . . { born Feb. 17, 1726–7 / bap. May 14, ——

4—Parents—James and Sarah.

Susannah . . . . . . born Oct. 6, 1747

5—Parents—Isaac and Elizabeth.

Sarah . . . . born Aug. 27, 1743

Isaac Walker . . . . . born Feb. 2, 1746

Ann . . . . born Feb. 14, 1749

Elizabeth . . . . . . born Oct. 30, 1751

Daniel . . . . born Dec. 31, 1752

Thomas . . . . born Mch. 9, 1754

William . . . . bap. Apl. 15, 1763

Julianna . . . . . . bap. May 7, 1772

6—Parents—Daniel and Mary Simons.

Mary . . . . born Nov. 26, 1756

Elizabeth . . . . . born Sep. 28, 1759

Esther . . . . bap. May 3, 1761

Anne . . . . { born Dec. 28, 1762 / bap. Feb. 6, 1763

James . . . . { born Oct. 10, 1764 / bap. Dec. 30, ——

Daniel . . . . { born May 11, 1766 / bap. July 14, ——

Lesesne, 6—Parents—Daniel and Mary Simons.

Sarah . . . . { born Mch. 2, 1768 / bap. Apl. 5, ——

Benjamin . . . . . . bap. Sep. 13, 1769

Isaac . . . . bap. Feb. 23, 1771

Peter . . . . bap. June 25, 1772

John . . . . bap. July 6, 1774

Thomas . . . . . . bap. Sep. 7, 1775

Maurice Keating . . . . bap. May 27, 1777

Leay—Parents—John and Mary Blake.

Blake . . . . { born Oct. 22, 1713 / bap. Nov. 8, ——

Lewis, 1—Parents—Charles and Elizabeth Horey.

Elizabeth . . . . . . born June 5, 1714

Charles . . . . born Sep. 9, 1715

Daniel . . . . born Aug. 9, 1717

2—Parents—Robert and Susannah.

Judith . . . . born Oct. 4, 1747

Susannah . . . . . . born June 27, 1750

Lea—Parents—Joseph and Catharine.

Joseph, / Robert Syer, } twins . . born July 27, 1722

Leroux, 1—Parents—James and Marian.

Anna . . . . born Mch. 28, 1723

James . . . . { born Dec. 10, 1725 / bap. Jan. 30, 1726

Mary Ann . . . . . { born Dec 25, 1727 / bap. Mch, 10, 1728

William . . . . . . born Apl, 17, 1729

John . . . . born Aug. 21, 1731

Judith Bugdin . . . . . born May 11, 1736

2—Parents—John and Elizabeth Vanal.

John . . . . bap. June 13, 1762

Livingston—Parents—William and Mary Fitch.

William . . . . bap. Apl. 26, 1752

Litz—Parents—Bernard and Mary Edon.

John . . . . bap. Mch. 27, 1757

Little—Parents—Aaron and ——

Elizabeth . . . . . . bap. Feb. 14, 1760

Logan, 1—Parents—Rev. Edward C. and Mary J.

John O'Hear . . . . { born June 26, 1867 / bap. Aug. —, ——

Martha Webb . . . . . bap. Aug. 2, 1868

Anna Legare . . . . . bap. Dec. 31, 1871

Edward Charles . . . { born Feb. 11, 1874 / bap. Apl. 5, ——

2—Parents—Roswell T. and Alice Plowden.

Roswell Plowden . . . bap. Mch. 29, 1868

Lucas—Parents—B. Simons and Mary L. Buist.

Emma Julia . . . . . . bap. Jan. 23, 1854

Catharine Simons . . . bap. Apl. 27, 1856

Martha Buist . . . . . bap. Feb. 6, 1859

Benjamin Simons . . . bap. Feb. 10, 1861

George Buist . . . . . bap. Apl. 24, 1863

George Buist—4 mos . . bap. Jan. 10, 1869

Elizabeth Buist . . . . bap. Apl. 23, 1871

M

Mauren—Parents—Lewis Paul and Mary.

Lewis . . . . { born Dec. 27, 1732 / bap. Feb. 4, 1733

Maxwell—Parents—James and Mary Simons.

Peter James . . . . . born Nov. 23, 1723

Elizabeth . . . . born July 2, 1725

Jane . . . . { born Feb. 23, 1732 / bap. Mch. 18, ——

Marbeuff, 1—Parents—Joseph and Hannah.

Joseph . . . . born Apl. 21, 1705

Esther . . . . born Oct. 12, 1707

Hannah . . . - . . . born Apl. 20, 1710

2—Parents—Joseph and Elizabeth Alston.

Elizabeth . . . . born Jan. 20, 1721-2

Joseph . . . . born Sep. 20, 1723

Mallet—Parents—James and Mary.

Mary Elizabeth . . . { born Dec. 30, 1724 / bap. Feb. 7, 1725

Marion, 1—Parents—James and Mary Bremar.

James . . . . born Nov. 24, 1751

Peter . . . . born Sep. 15, 1753

Paul . . . . born Aug. 29, 1757

2—Parents—Benjamin and Hester Bonneau.

Hester . . . . bap. Oct. 14, 1753

Anne . . . . bap. Sep. 21, 1755

Martha . . . . bap. Apl. 2, 1758

Elizabeth, ⎱ twins . . ⎰ born Feb. 28, 1760
Catharine, ⎰   ⎱ bap. Feb. 29, ——

3—Parents—John and Mary Sanders.

John . . . . bap. May 8, 1763

Maybank—Parents—Joseph and Hester Bonneau.

Hester . . . . bap. Apl. 26, 1761

Joseph . . . . bap. Mch. 17, 1765

Daniel, ⎱ . . . . . . bap. May 24, 1767
Andrew, ⎰ . . . . . . bap. —— — ——

Susannah . . . . . . bap. Dec. 10, 1769

Mary . . . . , ... bap. Mch. 28, 1773

Peter Bonneau . . . . bap. June 25, 1775

Martin, 1—Parents—John and Frances Ann.

Hamlin . . . . . . ⎰ born Dec. —, 1827
               ⎱ bap. Mch. 17, 1829

2—Parents—Samuel and Eliza.

William Henry . . . ⎰ born Oct. 26, 1844
               ⎱ bap. May 11, 1848

McDaniel—Parents—Daniel and Mary Lewis.

Ann . . . . born June 13, 1724

John . . . . born Mch. 6, 1725–6

McGregor—Parents—Duncan and Mary.

John . . . . born Sep. 28, 1726

McCulloch—Mary—adult . . . . . . bap. July 30, 1769

McDowell—Parents—George A. and Eliza.

William Behn . . . . ⎰ born —— —, 1835
               ⎱ bap. Nov. 25, ——

Mary Emma . . . . ⎰ born —— —, 1837
               ⎱ bap. May 21, ——

Merrill—Parents —— and ——

Three children . . . . . bap. Sep. 29, 1859

Mercer—Parents—George R. and Sarah C.

Elizabeth Arabella . . . bap. Aug. 18, 1872

Midleton—Parents—Thomas and Anna.

John . . . . { born Mch. 9, 1720–1 / bap. Apl. 13, ——

Miller, 1—Parents—Stephen and Martha Dutarque.

Mary . . . . born Mch. 22, 1747

Martha . . . . bap. Oct. 24, 1751

John . . . . bap. Dec. 7, 1759

Elizabeth . . . . bap. Mch. 27, 1763

2—Parents—Stephen and Mary Roche.

Stephen . . . . bap. Feb. 21, 1775

Micheau—Parents—Daniel and Mary Jennings.

Daniel . . . . bap. July 10, 1757

Miles—Parents—Thomas B. and Elizabeth, of Summerville.

Ann Waring . . . . . { born Apl. 30, 1847 / bap. Aug. 1, in ex.

Mitchel—Parents—John Adam and Catharine.

Catharine . . . . bap. Dec. 9, 1753

Mary . . . . bap. July 3, 1757

Monk—Parents—Thomas and Martha Aiken.

Sarah . . . . born Mch. 1, 1712–3

Mouzon—Parents—Lewis and ——

Isaac Anthony . . . . . bap. Dec. 11, 1748

James . . . . bap. Sep. 1, 1765

Samuel . . . . bap. Aug. 11, 1765

Ann . . . . bap. Feb. 1, 1769

Moore—Parents—John and Elizabeth.

Elizabeth . . . . . . { born June 21, 1755 / bap. Aug. 23, ——

Rachel . . . . { born Aug. 10, 1757 / bap. Oct. 6, ——

John Elias . . . . . . born Oct. 12, 1763

Mary . . . . { born Oct. 18, 1765 / bap. Dec. 8, ——

Sarah . . . . { born Mch. 30, 1767 / bap. July 12, ——

William . . . . bap. May 5, 1770

Elizabeth Margaret . . . bap. Mch. 22, 1772

Moore—Parents—John and Elizabeth

        Harriet . . . . $\begin{cases} \text{born June 17, 1773} \\ \text{bap. Dec. 29, ——} \end{cases}$

        Catharine . . . . . . bap. Feb. 16, 1777

Musgrove—Parents—John and Mary King.

        John . . . . $\begin{cases} \text{born Oct. 14, 1737} \\ \text{bap. Jan. 29, 1738} \end{cases}$

Muirhead—Parents—Murray and late Mrs. ——

        Rosa Elizabeth . . . . bap: May 12, 1872

Murray—Parents—Richard and ——

        Lilly Roxanne—infant . bap. Aug. 17, 1873

N

Nicholas—Parents—William and Mary Beech.

        William . . . . born Nov. 1, 1713

O

Oliver—Parents—James and Elizabeth.

        Elizabeth . . . . . . bap. Dec. 9, 1773

P

Pagitt, 1—Parents—John and Hannah.

        Thomas . . . . . . born Jan. 19, 1700–1

    2—Parents—Francis and ——

        Francis . . . . born Jan. 5, 1703–4

        Peter . . . . born Mch.10, 1706–7

        Juely . . . . born Apl. 3, 1709

        Mary . . . . born Aug.23, 1712

        John . . . . born Jan. 5, 1715–6

    3—Parents—Thomas and Anna.

        John . . . . born July 5, 1725

        Thomas . . . . July 28, 1727

Perdrieau—Parents—Benjamin and Mary.

        Peter . . . . $\begin{cases} \text{born Feb. 22, 1753} \\ \text{bap. July 29, ——} \end{cases}$

Plumer—Parents—Moses and Jean Verine, Mrs.

        Moses . . . . born Jan. 3, 1713–4

Pollock—Parents—Rev. John and Margaret.

        Mary . . . . born Oct. 24, 1710

        Joseph John . . . . . born Feb. 12, 1712–3

Poinsett—Parents—Joel and Susannah.

Peter . . . . born Sep. 20, 1719

Poitvine—Parents—Peter and ———

Peter . . . . { born Apl. 6, 1700 / bap. May 12, ———

Anthony . . . . . . { born Sep. 18, 1701 / bap. Oct. 1, ———

Susannah . . . . . . { born Sep. 17, 1703 / bap. Oct. 8, ———

Joseph . . . . { born Apl. 22, 1705 / bap. Apl. 29, ———

Marian . . . . { born Nov. 18, 1707 / bap. Jan. 14, 1708

Samuel . . . . { born Sep. 11, 1709 / bap. Oct. 2, ———

James . . . . . . { born Sep. 23, 1711 / bap. Oct. 21, ———

Judith . . . . { born Mch. 13, 1715 / bap. June 13, ———

Esther . . . . { born Dec. 8, 1716 / bap. Jan. 10, 1717

Anna . . . . { born Dec. 4, 1718 / bap. July 10, 1719

Isaac . . . . { born Jan. 8, 1720–1 / bap. Aug. 4, ———

Poole—Parents—William and Hannah Warbeuf.

William . . . . . . { born Sep. 15, 1730 / bap. Jan. 24, 1731

Poyas—Parents—John L. and Louisa.

John Lewis . . . . . { born Aug. 9, 1830 / bap. Apl. 11, 1831

Samuel Hamlin . . . { born Sep. 27, 1831 / bap. Apl. 11, 1832

Mary Magdalene . . . { born Aug. 19, 1835 / bap. Nov. 5, ———

John Lewis, ... bap. Nov. 5. 1835

Ann Eliza . . . . . { born May 22, 1840 / bap. May 13, 1843

Pring—Parents—William and Elizabeth Jennings.

John . . . . bap. May 27, 1764

Q

Quash, 1—Parents—Robert and Elizabeth.
Robert . . . . born Nov. 19, 1740
Susannah . . . . . . born Aug. 27, 1743
Elizabeth . . . . . . born Dec. 20, 1750
2—Parents—Robert and Constantia Hasell.
Sarah . . . . born Mch. 14, 1773

R

Ravenel—Parents—Dr. Edmund and Louisa.
Emma . . . . bap. May 6, 1838
Theodosia Ford . . . . bap. Oct. 13, 1839
Rembert—Parents—Isaac and Catharine.
Sarah Hamlin . . . { born —— ——
{ bap. Nov. 25, 1829
Mary Emmeline . . . { born Nov. 11, 1830
{ bap. Apl. 11, 1831
Eliza Jane . . . . . . born Nov. 7, 1835
Thos. Louis Tavel–ad'lt . bap. June 16, 1855
Reab—Parents—George and Charlotte M.
Alfred Huger . . . . { born Mch. 15, 1851
{ bap. Apl. 17, ——
Rivers—Parents—Maurice and Mary Savige.
Mary . . . . born July 13, 1725
Ann . . . . born Dec. 6, 1730
Roper—Parents—Jeremiah and Mary Warnock.
Mary . . . . born Dec. 5, 1714
Thomas . . . . born Jan. 25, 1716–7
Mary . . . . born Dec. 17, 1719
Elizabeth . . . . . . born Feb. 26, 1722–3
Jeremiah . . . . . . born Oct. 27, 1724
Rogers—Parents—James and Ann.
Mary . . . . born May 20, 1745
Roulain, 1—Parents—Abraham and Mary Ann Guerin.
James . . . . born Oct. 24, 1736
Abraham . . . . . . born Aug. 6, 1738
Mary . . . . born July 29, 1742

Roulain, 2—Parents—Daniel and Catharine.

Sarah . . . . bap. Mch 31, 1757

3—Parents—James and Susannah.

Ann . . . . bap. May 24, 1767
James . . . . , ... bap. Nov. 9, 1769
Mary Magdalene . . . . bap. July 14, 1771

Roche—Parents—Francis and Anna.

Mary . . . . bap. Apl. 1, 1732
Francis . . . . bap. Sep. 2, 1753
Anne . . . . bap. June 20, 1755
Patrick . . . . bap. May 28, 1757
Thomas . . . . bap. June 4, 1758
Jordan . . . . , . . . bap. Aug. 2, 1761
Anne . . . . bap. Aug. 12, 1761
Christopher . . . . . . bap. Feb. 27, 1763

Russ, 1—Parents—Jonathan and Elizabeth.

Jonathan . . . . born July 22, 1701
Marian . . . . born Oct. 28, 1702
Hezekiah . . . . born Apl. 12, 1704
Abijah . . . . born May 12, 1706
Keziah . . . . born Nov. 5, 1708
Elizabeth . . . . . . born Dec. 7, 1712
John . . . . born Dec. 20, 1718
Benjamin . . . . born Dec. 20, 1718

2—Parents—Jonathan and Martha Litten.

Elizabeth . . . . . . born July 6, 1723
Jonathan . . . . born Apl. 6, 1726
Wm. Litten . . . . . born Sep. 9, 1732
Elizabeth . . . . . . born Aug. 1, 1734
Abijah . . . . born Oct. 15, 1736
Martha . . . . born Dec. 28, 1740
Jacob . . . . born Nov. 10, 1744

3—Parents—Hezekiah and Catharine.

Hezekiah . . . . . . born Feb. 28, 1726–7
——— . . . . born Mch. 31, 1732

4—Parents—David and Catharine.

Catharine . . . . . . born Dec. 10, 1730

Russ, 5—Parents—Joseph and Elizabeth.

Elizabeth . . . . born Apl. 14, 1730

Joseph . . . . born Dec. 14, 1731

6—Parents—Benjamin and ———

Ann Elizabeth . . . . . born Feb. 16, 1777

Russel, 1—Parents—Jeremiah and Mary.

Elizabeth . . . . . . born Apl. 22, 1709

Joseph . . . . born Apl. 12, 1711

Mary . . . . born Feb. 10, 1712–3

2—Parents—James and Mary.

Peter . . . . bap. Apl. 1, 1752

Thomas Commander . . bap. June 2, 1754

——————— . . . . . bap. June 19, 1755

Rupp—Parents— ——— and Margaret.

Catharine . . . . bap. Sep. 14, 1777

S.

Sanders, 1—Parents—John and Sarah.

William . . . . born June 15, 1705

David . . . . born June 16, 1707

2—Parents—John and Mary.

John . . . . born Sept. 26, 1724

Thomas . . . . born Jan. 9, 1726

Sarah . . . . born Ap'l 20, 1729

William . . . . born July 20, 1731

Patience . . . . born Oct. 13, 1736

Hannah . . . . born Mch 29, 1739

Thomas Marion . . . . born Dec. 17, 1742

Sarah . . . . born Feb. 26, 1744–5

Mary . . . . born Nov. 3, 1746

Elizabeth . . . . born Dec. 12, 1748

Anne . . . . born May 5, 1754

John . . . . born Feb. 5, 1756

3—Parents—Thos. Martin and Mary Ann Mouzon.

John Martin . . . . { born Aug. 25, 1765
bap. Oct. 27, ———

4—Parents—Thos. Martin and Elizabeth Thomas.

Elizabeth . . . . born Jan. 28, 1769

Sanders, 5—Parents—John and Elizabeth.

John . . . . { born Jan. 19, 1825 / bap. Dec. 17, 1826

Thomas . . . . . . { born ——— 1827 / bap. Feb. 10, 1828

Susannah Constant . . { born Oct. 15, 1829 / bap Jan. 25, 1831

Samuel . . . . { born Sept. 16, 1831 / bap. Mch 25, 1832

Henry . . . . { ——— ——— / bap. Dec. 29, 1833

George Robert . . . { born ——— 1836 / bap. May 15, 1836

Francis Nathaniel . . . . ———————

6—Parents— ——— ——— and Mrs. W.

John William . . . . . bap. Aug. 31, 1858

7—Parents—Samuel and Emma.

Emily Louise, bap. in ex., 1860, by Rev. E. P.
and rec'd into Church Ap'l 28, 1872—E. C. L.

Mary Holmes . . . . . bap. Ap'l 5, 1862

Elizabeth Frances . . . bap. Ap'l 7, 1867

Clara Ann, 6 months . . bap. Jan. 31, 1869

John Samuel . . . . . bap. Ap'l 24, 1870

Edward Charles . . . . bap. Ap'l 28, 1872

Thomas Johnson . . . . bap. Ap'l 4, 1875

Robert Percy . . . . . bap. Jan. 14, 1877

Sams—Parents—Rev. J. Julius and Mary W.

Conway Whittle . . . . bap. Easter, 1862

Sallens, 1—Parents—Peter and Freelove.

Robert . . . . born May 22, 1714

Peter . . . . born Jan. 19, 1718-9

Thomas . . . . born May 15, 1721

Francis . . . . born Ap'l 24, 1726

2—Parents—Peter and . . . . . .

Susannah . . . . . . bap. Nov. 1, 1747

3—Parents—Robert and ———

Robert . . . . bap. Dec. 26, 1744

4—Parents—Robert and Elizabeth.

John . . . . born Mch 5, 1754

Elizabeth . . . . . . born May 2, 1756

6

Scanlan—Parents—Charles and Ruth,

Charles . . . . born Dec. 20, 1737

Scott—Parents—Joseph and Elizabeth Lesesne.

Joseph . . . . bap. Nov. 28, 1762

Seely—Parents—Rev. Richard S. and Elizabeth R.

Martha Emma . . . { born Dec. 11, 1851 / bap. Jan. 17, 1852

Sharp—Parents—Alexander and Mary Kayler.

John Alexander . . . . bap. Feb. 16, 1778

Shaw—Parents—Samuel and———

Mary . . . . bap. Jan. 12, 1752

William . . . . bap. Mch 7, 1767

Sinklair—Parents—Daniel and Ann.

Rebecca . . . . bap. Jan. 1, 1777

Simons, 1—Parents—Benjamin and Mary.

Peter . . . . born July 9, 1693

Samuel . . . . { born May 14, 1696 / bap. June 5, ———

Francis . . . . . . { born Dec. 7, 1697 / bap. Jan. 3, 1698

Hannah . . . . . . born Mch. 21, 1699-1700

Mary . . . . born Sep. 11, 1701

Elizabeth . . . . . . born Apl. 20, 1704

Martha . . . . { born Feb. 8, 1705–6 / bap. Apl. 14, ———

Esther . . . . { born June 1, 1710 / bap. June 21, ———

Judith . . . . . . { born Mch. 2, 1711–2 / bap. Apl. 21, ———

Benjamin . . . . . . { born June 12, 1713 / bap. June 19, ———

2—Parents—Peter and Magdalen.

Peter . . . . { born Nov. 24, 1717 / bap. Jan. 26, 1718

Esther . . . . { born Sep. 9, 1719 / bap. Oct. 18, ———

Anthony . . . . . . { born Dec. 25, 1721 / bap. Feb. 4, 1722

Simons, 3—Parents—Samuel and Elizabeth Bonneau.

Elizabeth . . . . born Dec. 28, 1725

Samuel . . . . born Oct. 3, 1727

Magdalen . . . . born Sep. 19, 1729

Henry . . . . born Aug. 25, 1733

Anthony . . . . born —— ——

——da . . . . { born —— —— bap. Aug. 9, 1747

4—Parents—Peter and ——

Esther . . . . { born May 12, 1740 bap. July 6, ——

5—Parents—Francis and Ann.

Ann . . . . born Sep. 5, 1725

Francis . . . . born Jan. 16, 1726–7

Hannah . . . . born Dec. 26, 1728

Esther . . . . born Dec. 30, 1730

6—Parents—Benjamin and Ann.

Benjamin . . . . born Sep. 10, 1737

Mary . . . . born Oct. 19, 1739

Peter . . . . born Feb. 16, 1740–1

Edward . . . . born July 19, 1742

Maurice . . . . born Jan. 26, 1743–4

Ann . . . . born Dec. 16, 1745

Elizabeth . . . . . . born July 11, 1747

Francis . . . . born Mch. 7, 1748–9

Rebecca . . . . born Mch. 30, 1750

Samuel . . . . born Oct. 12, 1751

Keating . . . . born Jan. 6, 1753

Rachel . . . . born Oct. 1, 1756

Robert . . . . born Jan. 3, 1758

Mary Hester . . . . . born July 11, 1759

James . . . . born Feb. 20, 1761

7—Parents—Francis and Elizabeth McGrigory.

Anne . . . . bap. Oct. 20, 1751

8—Parents—Samuel, Jr., and Frances.

Elizabeth . . . . . . bap. June 30, 1754

Frances . . . . bap. Nov. 10, 1755

Samuel . . . . bap. May 15, 1757

Peter . . . . bap Jan. 3, 1763

Simons, 9—Parents--Benjamin and Katharine Chicken.

Lydia . . . . bap. Sep. 16, 1765
Benjamin . . . . bap. Jan. 20, 1767
Edward . . . . bap. Oct. 28, 1770
Catharine . . . . bap. May 17, 1773
Mary . . . . bap. Aug. 29, 1777

Singletary, 1—Parents—Richard and Sarah.

Sarah . . . . born June 23, 1710
Richard . . . . born Nov. 1, 1713
Benjamin . . . . . . born Feb. 3, 1716-7
Sarah . . . . born June 25, 1719
Joseph . . . . born Jan. 14, 1721-2
Susan, } twins . . . . born Jan. 1, 1724-5
Anna }

2—Parents—Braton and Deborah Fewelling.

Mary . . . . born Feb. 20, 1712-3

3—Parents—John and Elizabeth.

Priscilla . . . . bap. Mch. 9, 1760

4—Parents—Thomas and Elizabeth Guerin.

Thomas . . . . bap. June 25, 1762
Anna . . . . bap, Dec. 13, 1769

Smith—Parents—James and Betty.

Sarah . . . . bap. May 17, 1773
Celia . . . . bap. May 17, 1773
Amelia . . . . bap. May 17, 1773
———— . . . . bap. —— ——
Mary Ann Elizabeth—a
child . . . . bap. —— 1853

Stewart—Parents—James and Sarah.

Sarah . . . . born —— 1730
Mary . . . . { born Dec. 23, 1731
{ bap. Feb. 20, 1732

Stinson—Parents—Thomas and Hester Bourdeaux.

James Simon . . . . . bap. Aug. 3, 1769

Stone—Parents—Joseph and ————

Sarah . . . . bap. Sep. 7, 1746
Elizabeth . . . . . . bap. Dec. 2, 1753

Stutts—Parents—W. W. and E. M.

Arthur Eugene—2 yrs . bap. July 30, 1876

Mary Ella—infant . . . bap. July 30, 1876

St. Martin—Parents—John and Sarah.

Mary . . . . born Feb. 3, 1703–4

Anna . . . . born Nov. 20, 1706

John . . . . born July 25, 1710

Sarah . . . . . . { born May 25, 1712 / bap. June 29, ——

Hannah . . . . born Dec. 13, 1713

Syer—Parents—Robert and Anna.

Grace . . . . born Feb. 5, 1703–4

Catharine . . . . born July 9, 1705

Mary . . . . born Nov. 29, 1707

Syme—Parents—Dr. John and Margaret Ashby.

John . . . . { born Nov. 18, 1761 / bap. Apl. —, 1762

T.

Tart, 1—Parents—Nathan and Sarah Sanders.

Nathan . . . . born Mch. 21, 1748

Mary . . . . born Nov. 21, 1754

2—Parents—Nathan and Elizabeth Garden.

Sarah Amelia . . . . { born Feb. 1, 1774 / bap. Mch 27, ——

Elizabeth . . . . . . { born Mch 12, 1776 / bap. Ap'l 20, ——

Nathan . . . . bap. Aug. 17, 1777

Tamplett, 1—Parents—Peter and Christian.

Peter . . . . born Jan. 20, 1727–8

2—Parents—Peter and Izabella.

Stephen . . . . . . { born May 29, 1733 / bap. Aug. 5, ——

Taylor—Parents—Peter and ——

Ann Elizabeth . . . . . bap. Feb. 6, 1777

Threadcraft—Parents—Thomas and Mary.

Mary . . . . { born Jan. 18, 1711–12 / bap. June 29, ——

Thomas, 1—Parents—Samuel and ———
              Edward . . . . bap. Feb. 17, 1745
          2—Parents—Samuel and Elizabeth Ashby.
              Anne . . . . bap. Ap'l 29, 1753
              Elizabeth Ashby . . . . bap. Feb. 9, 1755
              Andrew . . . . bap. July 12, 1761
          3—Parents—John and Deborah.
              Deborah . . . . . . $\begin{cases} \text{born June 26, 1763} \\ \text{bap. Dec. ———} \end{cases}$
              Henrietta Judith . . . $\begin{cases} \text{born Nov. 6, 1765} \\ \text{bap. June 7, 1766} \end{cases}$
              John . . . . $\begin{cases} \text{born June 29, 1767} \\ \text{bap. Oct. 6, ———} \end{cases}$
          4—Parents—Samuel and Ann.
              Joseph . . . . bap. Mch 17, 1764
          5—Parents—Edward and Ann.
              Mary . . . . bap. Dec. 12, 1771
          6—Parents—Thomas W. and Elizabeth H., Abbeville.
              Elizabeth Ann . . . $\begin{cases} \text{born July 15, 1847} \\ \text{bap. Oct. 4, ———} \end{cases}$
Tidyman—Parents—Philip and Hester.
              Philip . . . . bap. May 11, 1778
Tiencken—Parents—John and L. Anna Poyas.
              Jno. Henry, under 2 y'rs . bap. July 6, 1876
              Sam'l Hamlin   "   . bap. July 6, 1876
Tousigere—Parents—Stephen and Martha.
              Elizabeth . . . . . . bap. May 3, 1752
Townsend—Parents—William and Sarah Bedon.
              William . . . . . . bap. July 10, 1752
Toomer—Parents—Henry B. and Ann E.
              Henrietta . . . . . $\begin{cases} \text{born Oct. 13, 1845} \\ \text{bap. May 3, 1846} \end{cases}$
Tresvan—Parents—Theodorus and Martha Scriven, Mrs.
              Theodorus . . . . . . born Ap'l 20, 1722
              Martha . . . . born Aug. 25, 1724
              Daniel . . . . born June 6, 1726
Tyrrel—Edmund H. . . . . bap. Mch 26, 1863

V.

Vanderhorst—Parents—Joseph and Jane Follingsby.

John . . . . bap. Mch. 15, 1761

John . . . . bap. June 7, 1763

Valley—Parents—Thomas and Elizabeth.

Thomas . . . . { born Oct. 25, 1732 / bap. Feb. 25, 1733

Verine, 1—Parents—Jeremiah and Jean.

Jeremiah . . . . born Jan. 6, 1706–7

Mary . . . . born Jan. 23, 1709-10

2—Parents—Jeremiah and Mary.

William . . . . born Nov. 3, 1729

Elis . . . . { born Nov. 14, 1731 / bap. Mch. 5, 1732

Verone—Florence—infant . . . . . . bap. Mch. 19, 1862

Venning, 1—Parents—William Lucas and Olivia Haskell.

Eliza Lucilla . . . . . bap. Apl. 24, 1856

2—Parents—Wm. Carey and Emma C.

Jonah Murrell, 7 years . . bap. July 5, 1874

Samuel Clandius, 3 years . bap. July 5, 1874

Julia Mary, 4 months . . bap. July 5, 1874

Ida Bee . . . . { born June 12, 1882 / bap. June 16, ——

3—Parents—Robert Mc., and Eliza, of Mt. Pleasant.

Richard Septimus . . { born July 11, 1840 / bap. Oct. 25, 1843

Videau—Parents—Henry and Ann.

Elizabeth . . . . born Jan. 6, 1733–4

Mary . . . . born Sep. 17, 1737

Peter . . . . born Oct. 27, 1743

Henry Joseph . . . . . born Dec. 4, 1744

W.

Wastecoat—Parents—John and Elizabeth.

John . . . . born July 9, 1708

Joseph . . . . born Feb. 1, 1712–3

Mary . . . . born Sept. 27, 1710

Warnock, 1—Parents—Andrew and Mary.

Judith . . . . born Oct. 7, 1704
Joseph . . . . born Ap'l 7, 1708
Andrew . . . . born May 11, 1710
Rachel . . . . born Feb. 14, 1712–3
Samuel . . . . born Sep. 23, 1714
John . . . . born Mch 3, 1716–7
Martha . . . . born Ap'l 23, 1718

2—Parents—Abraham and Thomozon.

Thomozon (da.) . . . . born Dec. 14, 1724
Abraham . . . . born May 21, 1726
Mary . . . . born June 4, 1732

3—Parents—Joseph and Mary.

Mary . . . . born July 20, 1732

4—Parents—Andrew and Thomozon.

Andrew . . . . born Sep. 7, 1741
Thomozon . . . . . born Dec. 6, 1742
Abraham . . . . born Ap'l 17, 1744
Rachel . . . . born Nov. 11, 1745
John . . . . born Feb. 18, 1747

5—Parents—Joseph and Ann.

Mary Martha . . . . . bap. May 4, 1778

Wagner—Parents—Effingham and Emma B., of Mt. Pleasant.

Eugene Fronty . . . { born Ap'l 1, 1843
                    { bap. July 12, 1845

Clarence . . . . . . { born Mch 2, 1845
                     { bap. July 12, 1845

Watts, 1—Parents—Thomas and Elizabeth.

Thomas . . . . born May 25, 1723

John . . . . . . { born Aug. 18, 1725
                 { bap. Jan. 11, 1729-30

David . . . . . . { born Oct. 15, 1729
                  { bap. Jan. 11, ——

2—Parents—David and Elizabeth.

Anne . . . . bap. Oct. 12, 1761
Margaret . . . . bap. Feb. 19, 1764
Elizabeth . . . . . . bap. May 26, 1766
Mary Rachel . . . . . bap. Ap'l 24, 1774

Watts, 3—Parents—Thomas and Hester.

Hester . . . . bap. Mch 4, 1765

Walter—Parents—E. Wilmot and Sarah P., of Charleston.

Theodosia . . . . . { born Feb. 11, 1843 / bap. July 3, ——

Wells, 1—Parents—Edgar and Lidia Roper.

William . . . . . . born May 23, 1710

Samuel . . . . . . born May 22, 1712

Joseph . . . . born June 18, 1714

2—Parents—William and Frances Dubois.

Henry . . . . . . bap. Feb. 5, 1776

Frances . . . . . . bap. Oct. 7, 1777

Welsh—Parents—John George and Margaret Ettering.

Mary Magdalene . . . bap. Dec. 31, 1769

John Philip . . . . . bap. Feb. 25, 1770

Westendorf—Parents—James and Eliza J.

Lizzie Rembert . . . . bap. Mch. 5, 1871

Weekley—Parents—Dr. —— and ——

Ann Elizabeth . . . . . bap. Feb. 16, 1868

John Francis Sanders . . bap. Feb. 16, 1868

Nathaniel Washington . bap. Feb. 16, 1868

White, 1—Parents—John and Sarah Roddam.

William . . . . bap. Sep. 6, 1775

Sarah . . . . bap. Nov. 26, 1777

2—Parents—John and Elizabeth.

Mary . . . . bap. Dec. 7, 1775

John . . . . bap. Nov. 21, 1777

Wigfall, 1—Parents—Samuel and ——

Benjamin . . . . . . born —— ——

2—Parents—John and Constantia.

Constantia . . . . . { born —— —— / bap. Aug. 2, 1761

Catharine . . . . . . { born Apl. 7, 1762 / bap. Dec. 25, ——

Samuel . . . . { born Dec. 28, 1766 / bap. Apl. 23, 1767

Thomas . . . . bap. Sep. 24, 1769

Wigfall, 3—Parents—Joseph and Susannah Durand.

Elias . . . . bap. Apl. 7, 1776

4—Parents—John and Constantia.

William . . . . . . $\begin{cases} \text{born —— ——} \\ \text{bap. June 10, 1776} \end{cases}$

Sarah . . . . . . $\begin{cases} \text{born Jan. 16, 1778} \\ \text{bap. June 28, ——} \end{cases}$

5—Parents—John A. and Susan M.

Harriet Moore . . . . $\begin{cases} \text{born —— ——} \\ \text{bap. Apl. 27, 1843} \end{cases}$

John Nowell . . . . $\begin{cases} \text{born Oct. 3, 1844} \\ \text{bap. July 13, 1845} \end{cases}$

John A., adult . . . . . born Oct. 3, 1791

Wienges—Parents—Joseph and Lucinda A.

John L. Poyas . . . . $\begin{cases} \text{born July 31, 1842} \\ \text{bap. May 13, 1843} \end{cases}$

Williams, 1—Parents—John J. and Esther, of Abbeville.

John Drum . . . . . $\begin{cases} \text{born May 10, 1841} \\ \text{bap. Oct. 7, 1842} \end{cases}$

Ann Eliza . . . . . . $\begin{cases} \text{born Aug. 14, 1842} \\ \text{bap. Oct. 7, 1842} \end{cases}$

2—Parents—Daniel and Elizabeth.

Mary . . . . bap. Apl. 10, 1764

Elizabeth . . . . . . bap. May 4, 1772

Mary . . . . bap. July 26, 1774

Witten—Parents—Thomas and Elizabeth Stanley.

Thomas . . . . born Dec. 18, 1719

Edward . . . . born Dec. 25, 1721

James . . . . $\begin{cases} \text{born May 23, 1727} \\ \text{bap. June 25, ——} \end{cases}$

Wood, 1—Parents—William and Sarah.

Abram . . . . bap. Sep. 2, 1753

2—Parents—Moses and Sarah.

Sarah . . . . bap. June 20, 1755

Wright, 1—Parents—William and Sarah Howard.

Mary . . . . born Feb. 7, 1713-4

William . . . . born Dec. 31, 1717

Thomas . . . . . . born Dec. 25, 1722

Wright, 2—Parents—Jonathan and Lovelace.

Sarah Isabella, 8 mos. . . bap. Aug. 17, 1873
Florence Webbie, 3 yrs. . bap. Aug. 17, 1873
Peter Friendly, 6 yrs. . . bap. Aug. 17, 1873
Thomas Benjamin, 10 yrs..bap. Aug. 17, 1873
Anne Matilda, infant . . bap. May 29, 1877

Y.

Yates—Parents—Joseph and Susan.

Clarence . . . . . . { born Feb. 4, 1850
{ bap. the same day.

" He that believeth and is baptized, shall be saved."
ST. MARK xvi. 16.

REGISTER

OF

DEATHS AND BURIALS.

DEATHS AND BURIALS.

I am forgotten as a dead man out of mind. PSALM XXXI, 12.

A.

Addy, Martha N., *b.* Nov. 27, 1842, age, 19, Brick Church.

Addison, Joseph, Esq., *d.* Sept. 30, 1817, age, 47, Brick Church.

Joseph B., *d.* Mch. 9, 1849, age, 24, Brick Church.

Akin, Sarah, *b.* June 6, 1750.

James, Esq., *b.* Oct. 31, 1758.

Alston, Peter, *b.* April 16, 1748.

John, son of Dr. E. F., *b.* Sept. 7, 1873, age, 2, Old Ruins.

Anderson, J. J. Mrs., *d.* Oct. 26, 1874, age, 37, Brick Church

Ashby, John, Esq., *d.* Nov. 30, 1716.

Constancia, his widow, *d.* Jan. 20, 1720

John, Esq., *d.* Mch., 1729.

Thomas, Col., *b.* Nov. 5, 1750.

Thomas—

John, *b.* Apl. 16, 1758.

Ashton, Joseph, *d.* June 27, 1737.

B.

Baker, Henry, son of Eben'r and Han'h, *b.* May 17, 1712.

Miles, *d.* Dec. 29, 1732.

Backes, Abel, *b.* Aug. 24, 1882, age, 37, Methodist Church.

Batchelor, David, *d.* March 22, 1710.

Hannah, *d.* Mch. 1, 1716-7.

Ball, Sarah, wife of Thomas, *d.* Jan. 6, 1718-9.

Thomas, son of Thomas, *d.* April 4, 1723.

Ball, Lydia, wife of Elias, b. April 3, 1765, Childsbury.

    Isaac, b. Apl. 2, 1867, age, 70.

Babbitt, Henry, son of P. T., b. Oct. 25, 1847, infant, St. Paul's, Charleston.

Besselleu, Philip A., son of Philip A., b. March 19, 1778.

Beresford, Sarah, wife of Richard, Esq., d. Nov. 28, 1712, b. 29, age, 21, Brick Church.

    Dorothy, wife (2d) of Richard, Esq., d. June 20, 1720.

    *Richard, Esq., d. Mch. 17, 1721–2.

    Richard, Jr., son of R. and D., d. Nov. 17, 1723.

Beech, Mary, d. Chris. and Mary, b. Jan. —, 1711–2.

    Christopher, b. May 25, 1712.

    Richard, b. April 11, 1713.

Beasely, Catharine, b. Jan. 17, 1836, age, 7.

Bird, Mary, b. Nov. 7, 1755, Kainhoy.

    Robert, b. Nov. 2, 1768, Dr. Mayer's plantation.

    ———, b. April 7, 1830, age, 34.

Black, Mary, b. Oct. 31, 1770.

Blunt, ——, Mrs., b. Aug. 11, 1861, Pompion Hill.

Bochett, Nicholas, d. April 15, 1733.

    Nicholas, b. Nov. 21, 1743, his plantation.

    Frances, wife of Peter, b. Feb. 1, 1769.

    Peter, b. April 24, 1772, his plantation.

    Samuel, b. May 4, 1772, Pompion Hill.

Bonneau, Anthony, son of Ant'y, Jr., d. April 16, 1733.

    Peter, b. Aug. 29, 1748, Pompion Hill.

    Anthony, son of Ant'y, b. Aug. 3, 1750.

    Henry, b. Sep. 21, 1759.

    Margaret, widow, b. April 4, 1761.

    Elias, Jr., b. Dec. 1, 1762.

    Mary, wife of Elias, b. Sep. 5, 1770.

    Elias, b. July 13, 1773, Pompion Hill.

Bourdin, Mary, d. Michael, b. Dec. 30, 1745.

Bonny, ——, wife of Thomas, b. April 19, 1746.

Bourdeaux, James, Sr., b. Mch. 8, 1767, plantation.

    Mary Ann, b. Sep. —, 1767, age, 77.

---

* Founder of the Beresford Bounty School.

Bosh, John F., *b.* Aug. 25, 1882, age, 56, Methodist Church.
Brunning, Henry, *d.* Oct. 7, 1881, age, 45, Brick Church.
Bremar, Solomon, *d.* Jan. 27, 1720–1.
    Peter, *d.* Aug. 3, 1732.
    Hester, d. Francis, *b.* Oct. 10, 1745.
    Mary, wife of James, *b.* Dec. 9, 1747.
    James, *b.* Mch. 17, 1748–9, plantation.
Bruce, ——, wife of Dr. Wm., *b.* Oct. 14, 1749.
    William, *b.* April 18, 1752, Pompion Hill.
Bryan, John, *b.* —, 1810, infant, Pompion Hill.
    Lydia, wife of John, *b.* Jan. 29, 1813, age 86, Pompion Hill.
    Eliza, *b.* —, 1821, Pompion Hill.
Burcham, Samuel, *d.* Oct. 3, 1718.
Buckley, Grace, *d.* Feb. 16, 1721–2.
Buckle, John, B. B. S., *b.* May 1, 1749.
Burnham, Thos. May, B. B. S., son of Thos., *b.* Aug. 8, 1761.

C.

Carrol, Sarah, *b.* Sep. 12, 1771.
Caradeux, Louisa Agatha, *d.* May 4, 1802, age, 15, Brick Ch.
    Achille, Jr., *d.* Sep. 15, 1804, age, 15, Brick Church.
    Maria L. Chateaublond, *d.* Sep. 24, 1807, age, 61, Brick Church.
    *John B., Gen'l, *d.* May 25, 1810, age, 68, Brick Ch.
    John Baptiste, *d.* Sep. 26, 1812, age, 2 mos., Brick Church.
    John B. U. L., *d.* Nov. 18, 1820, age, 34, Brick Ch.
    John, *b.* Nov. 6, 1836, age, 30, Brick Church.
    John B., *d.* Nov. 11, 1836, age. 22.
Cason, Minnie, *b.* Nov. 18, 1872, age 6 mos., Irishtown.
Chovin, Mary, wife of Alex., *b.* Feb. 22, 1775.
Cleave, Nathan, *d.* April 27, 1761.
Clute, Gertrude O., d. Rev. R. F., *d.* Aug. 25, 1882, age, 8⅓, Methodist Church.

---

* Commander-in-Chief of the French army during the revolt in St. Domingo, 1798.

7

Cox, Mary, b. Nov. 3, 1834.

E., b. June 5, 1863, age, 67.

Thomas C., b. May 10, 1869, age, 37, Methodist Church.

Lorenzo, Mrs., b. April 12, 1873, age, 45, Brick Church.

Cotchett, M. A., Mrs., b. Nov. 2, 1857, Pompion Hill.

Coward, James, b. Feb. 11, 1859, age, 62, Fishbrook.

Cook, Thomas, b. Nov. 22, 1711.

John, Esq., b. Nov. 6, 1744.

Collins, Anne, wife of Jona, b. Mch. 16, 1744-5.

Jonathan, b. Nov. 8, 1761.

Mary, widow of Jona, b. Dec. 21, 1773.

Codner, wife of Chas., b. Feb. 8, 1745.

Coyte, Hercules, b. April 23, 1750.

Combe, John, b. Dec. 8, 1770.

Martha, b. Dec. 27, 1770.

Curtiss, Martha, b. Oct. 28, 1727.

D.

Daniel, Sarah, wife of Daniel, d. July 31, 1721.

*Robert, Esq., b. June 4, 1732.

Elizabeth d. Robt. & Eliz'h, b. July 17, 1763, Brick Ch.

Robert Litten, son R. and E, b. Oct. 31, 1764, Brick Ch.

Danzy, Richard, b. Mch. 1, 1725-6.

William, son Rd. and Sarah, d. Mch. 19, 1725-6.

Darby, Elizabeth, d. Capt. Michael and Elizabeth, d. Feb. 19, 1731.

Elizabeth, wf. Capt. Michael, d. Mch. 3, 1732-3.

Judith, wf. Capt. Michael, d. Nov. 5, 1734.

Michael, Capt., d. Feb. —, 1739-40.

Michael Videau, b. June 17, 1750.

Dannelly, Mary, b. Dec. 10, 1749, Brick Church.

Anne, b. Dec. 15, 1749, Brick Church.

Edward, b. Dec. 24, 1749, Brick Church.

Margaret, widow Ed., d. Feb. 21, 1765.

Dallas, Walter, b. Dec. 17, 1749.

Dean, Nathaniel, b. Oct. 20, 1773.

---

*Ex-Governor of the Province.

DeLonguemar, Nicholas, *b*. Jan. 15, 1711–12.
        Mary, widow Nicholas, *b*. Oct. 22, 1712.
Dearington, Thomas, Sr., *b*. Jan. 13, 1763.
        Eliza, *d*. Nov. 5, 1767.
        Patience, widow Thos., *b*. Nov. 18, 1771.
DuPre, James, *b*. July, 7, 1712.
DuRant, Jean, d. Henry and Anna, *b*. Sep. 18, 1716.
Durand, Lévi, Rev. *b*. Mch. 22, 1765, Childsbury.
Dubois, Jasper, *b*. Oct. 24, 1748.
        John, *b*. Mch. 29, 1763, Jaudon's Plantation.
        James, *b*. Jan. 25, 1772, Jaudon's Plantation.
Duke, Thomas, *b*. Mch. 1, 1755.
Dutarque, Joseph, son Lewis and Xtn., *d*. June 12, 1721.
        Mary, d. Lewis, *d*. June 15, 1721.
        Christiana, wife Lewis, *d*. Feb. 6, 1732.
        Lewis, *b*. Oct. 11, 1748, Plantation.
        Joseph, son John, *b*. Oct. 3, 1750.
        Christiana, d. John, *b*. Feb. 19, 1752.
        Noah, son John, *b*. July 17, 1761.
        John, Sr., *d*. Nov. 24, 1766, Plantation.
        Judith, d. John, Jr. and Mary, *b*. Mch. 21, 1767,
          Plantation.
        Mary, wife John, *b*. Oct. 11, 1767, Plantation.
Dutart, Adaline Rebecca, d. James, *b*. Jan. 28, 1860, Brick Ch.
        John, *b*. Feb. 14, 1864, age 21, Brick Church.
        James E., *b*. Mch. 25, 1876, Brick Church.
Dulette, Kate Hampton, *b*. Dec. 29, 1854, Brick Church.
Dwight, Daniel, Rev., *b*. Mch. 29, 1748, Childsbury.
Dyzart, George, *d*. Sept. 21, 1732.

E.

Edwards, John, *b*. Feb., 1776.
        William, *d*. Aug. 14, 1800, age 1, Brick Church.
        Isaac, Esq., *d*. June 17, 1813, age 53, Brick Church.
        Daniel C., *b*. Dec. 18, 1836, age 39.
Elliot, Thomas, son Thos., *b*. Mch. 22, 1745–6.
Elder, Charlotte, wife Dr. Thos., *b*. Feb. 15, 1775, Brick Ch.

Elfe, Eliza Slann, *b*. May 1, 1862, Brick Church.
    Martha Ann, *b*. Feb. 27, 1870, age 81, Brick Church.
    Eliza J., wife George, *b*. July 13, 1880, age 64, Brick Ch.
    George, *b*. Nov. 17, 1880, age 83, Brick Church.
    Clement Augustus, son George, *b*. Feb. 11, 1881, age
       26, Brick Church.

F.

Farmer, Mr. Rev., *b*. Sep. 12, 1769, Childsbury.
Fitzgerald, Susannah, *d*. April 20, 1737.
Floyd, Lilly Collins, d. Mrs. A. E. *b*. Aug. 12, 1869, age 2,
    Brick Church.
Flagg, Henry Collins, Dr., *d*. April 1, 1801, age 56, Brick Ch.
    Rachel, widow, Dr., *d*. Dec. 27, 1839, age 84, Brick Ch.
Fogartie, Lidia, d. John and Mary, *d*. June 12, 1716.
    Mary, wf. David, *b*. Dec. 3, 1757.
    ——. widow, *b*. Aug. 17, 1777, Brick Church.
    Stephen D., *b*. Dec. 11, 1826, age 42.
    Stephen D., *b*. Dec. 7, 1873, age 52, Brick Church.
Follingsly, ——— s. William, *b*. July 13, 1752.
    Joseph, s. William, *b*. Sep. 15, 1757.
Ford, Mary, *b*. Oct. 10, 1755, Kainhoy.
Fordham, Richard, *d*. June 4, 1823, age 80, Brick Church.
    Mary, Mrs. *d*. Dec. 10, 1832, age 82, Brick Church.
    Hannah Poinsett, *b*. April 30, 1855, age 64, Br. Ch.
Frewin, Francis, s. Chas. and Ann, *b*. Mch. —, 1769.

G.

Garden, Amy, wf. Rev. Alex., *d*. Dec. 7, 1763, Charleston.
    Susannah D., wf. Dr. Alex., *d*. Oct. 25, 1789, age 20,
       Brick Church.
    Sarah, wf. Dr. Alex., *d*. Dec. 25, 1794, age 26, Br. Ch.
    Henry, s. Dr. Alex., age 24 days, Brick Church.
    Daniel Lesesne, s. Dr. Alex., age 29 days, Brick Ch.
Gibson, Anne, d. Robert, *b*. Oct. 13, 1769.
    Jane, wf. Robert, *b*. Jan. 14, 1770.
Glen, Alex., s. Wm., Jr., *b*. Aug. 20, 1776.

Goddard, Mary, *d.* April 20, 1731.
Gray, s. Henry, *b.* Jan. 20, 1752.
      Mary, d. Henry, *b.* Sep. 25, 1757.
Guerin, Lewis, s. Isaac and Martha, *d.* Feb. 19, 1735.
      Elizabeth, *b.* Sep. —, 1750.
      John, *b.* Nov. 9, 1756.
      Sarah, wf. Robert, *b.* Jan. 7, 1764, Brick Church.
      Peter, *d.* April 12, 1765.
      ———, *b.* July 15, 1766, plantation.
      Magdalene, wf. Henry, *b.* Nov. 28, 1769.
      Henry, *b.* April —, 1772, old plantation.
      Robert, *b.* April 8, 1776.
      Samuel, *b.* Dec. 27, 1777.

H.

Hamilton, Bridget, wf. Arch'd, *d.* Sep. 2, 1727.
Hayes, Anne, *b.* Jan. 21, 1748, Pompion Hill.
Hays, Charles, Sr., *d.* Jan. 9, 1732-3.
      Charles, *d.* April 4, 1735.
Harris, Richard, *d.* Aug. 1732.
      Hannah, *d.* Oct. 22, 1732.
Hasell, Ann, d. Rev. Thomas, *d.* June 16, 1733.
      Thomas, Rev., *b.* Oct. 10, 1744, Pompion Hill.
      Thomas, s. Rev., *b.* Sep. 3, 1745.
      Elizabeth, widow Rev. Thomas, *b.* Mch. 21, 1746-7.
      Andrew, s. Rev. Thomas, *d.* Sep. 11, 1763.
Hartley, Frances, d. Stephen, *b.* July 12, 1750.
Hales, James, *b.* Jan. 22, 1768, Brick Church.
      Eleanor, *b.* Aug. 1, 1777, Brick Church.
Harleston, John, *b.* Nov. 29, 1767, Childsbury.
      Nicholas, *b.* Jan. 28, 1768, Childsbury.
      Edward, *b.* Feb. 13, 1871, age 74, Strawberry.
Hamlin, Alfred Huger, *b.* Dec. 27, 1834, age 7 months.
      Elizabeth, *d.* Feb. 14, 1840, age 2, Brick Church.
      Samuel, *d.* Dec. 21, 1848, age 77 Brick Church.
      Harriet, *b.* Sep. 9, 1862, age 86.
      W. E., *d.* July 5, 1865, age 24, Brick Church.

Hamlin, George McDowell, *b.* Oct. 29, 1873, age 42, Br. Ch.

Theodore A., *b.* May 2, 1877, age 2, Meth. Church.

Hall, Ann Eliza d. John and Mary, *b.* Nov. 27, 1849, age 1.

J. T., *b.* Oct. 12, 1867, age 70, Brick Church.

Hart, Amelia, d. J. R., *b.* Nov. 27, 1876, infant, Brick Church.

Heath, Thomas, *d.* Oct. 20, 1845, age 44, Hob-Caw, Christ Ch.

Henly, Mary, *d.* —— 1734.

Hetherington, John, *b.* Aug. 12, 1769, Brick Church.

Howard, Anna, d. Edward and Letties, *d.* Mch. 3, 1721–2.

Letties, wf. Edward, *d.* Sep. 18, 1727.

How, Elizabeth, d. Robert, *d.* Feb. 11, 1731–2.

Judith, d. Robert, *d.* Aug. 28, 1736.

Susannah Elizabeth, wf. Robert, *d.* Aug. 28, 1736.

Isaac, s. Robert, *d.* July 6, 1739.

William, s. Robert, *d.* Aug. 14, 1743.

Elizabeth, wf. Robert, *b.* Mch. 16, 1748.

Elizabeth, d. Robert, *b.* Aug. 3, 1750.

Robert, *b.* July 15, 1765, Brick Church.

Horey, ——, s. Daniel, *b.* Mch. 26, 1767, Dutarque Place.

Huger, Daniel, of St. John's, *b.* Dec. 8, 1754.

Alfred, Jr., (Hagan), *b.* Dec. 26, 1856, age 34, Limer'k.

I

Ingraham, Robert s. Wm. P. and H., *d.* Jan. 24, 1848, 7 mos. Pompion Hill.

Wm. Postell, Sr., *d.* Feb. 28, 1869, Pompion Hill.

Hannah H., *d.* Oct. 14, 1857, Pompion Hill.

Wm. Postell, Jr., *d.* Mch 14, 1875, age 25, Pompion Hill.

J

Jaudon, Mary, *b.* June 25, 1776.

Jefferds, John, *b.* Jan. 11, 1752.

Daniel, s. Daniel, *b.* Sept. 1770.

Jeffords, Elizabeth, Mrs., *b.* Jan. 13, 1873, age 76, St. Michael's.

Jenkins, Sarah Ann, *d.* July 6, 1839, age 2, Brick Church.

*Johnson, Nathan'l, Rt. Hon. Sir, *b.* July 2, 1712, Silk Hope.

*Ex-Governor of the Province.

Johnston, Robert, *b.* Aug. 25, 1745.
David, *b.* Ap'l 11, 1752.
Elizabeth, d. Rob't and Elizabeth, *b.* Oct. 12, 1763, Brick Church.
Sarah, d. Rob't and Elizabeth, *b.* Oct. 31, 1764, Brick Church.
Lydia, d. Rob't and Elizabeth, *b.* June 17, 1775.
Joel, John, *b.* Dec. 22, 1771.
Hester, *b.* Oct. 14, 1773.

K

Karwon, Mary, wf. Thos., *b.* Aug. 8, 1773.
Thomas, *b.* July 16, 1829, Pompion Hill.
Kennedy, Rebecca, wf. And., *b.* Ap'l 7, 1847, age 40, Brick Church.
King, Richard, *b.* Feb. 16, 1711–12.
Robert, Esq., *d.* Nov. 19, 1722.
Mrs., wf. J. K. (M. D.) *b.* Dec. 25, 1828, age 48.
Thomas, *b* July 10, 1859, age 3, Pompion Hill.
Kugley, David, *b.* Ap'l 4, 1843, age 32, Methodist Church.

L

Lawrence, Jonathan, s. Thos. H. and Helen (N. Y.), *d.* Oct. 18, 1782, age 33, Brick Church.
Robert D., Esq., *d.* May 26, 1807, age 28, Brick Church.
Sarah, Mrs., *d.* Mch 9, 1842, age 82, Brick Church.
Lane, —— *b.* Aug. 13, 1761, Quash Plantation.
Lapase, infant of Robt. and Laura, *b.* Sept 9, 1859, Brick Ch.
Lachicotte, Julius, *b.* Jan. 2, 1861, Brick Church.
Lesesne, Elizabeth, wf. Isaac, *d.* July 10, 1721.
William, s. Isaac, *d.* Aug. 16, 1764.
Isaac, *b.* Mch 18, 1772, Daniel's Island.
Elizabeth, wid. Isaac, *b.* Aug. —, 1775.
Daniel, *d.* Nov. 30, 1782, age 64, Brick Church.
Mary, wf. Daniel, *d.* May 15, 1791, age 51, Brick Ch.
Thomas, *d.* Aug. 30, 1813, age 38, Brick Church.
Peter, *b.* Ap'l 21, 1837, age 64.

Leitz, Peter, s. Bernard, *b.* Mch 29, 1770.
Lea, Catharine, wf. Joseph, *d.* July 29, 1722.
 Joseph, s. Joseph, *d.* Aug. 28, 1724.
 Robert Syer, s. Joseph, *d.* Sept. 8, 1724.
Leneed, Nicholas, *d.* May 18, 1737.
Leroux, Anna, d. James, *b.* Ap'l 6, 1723.
Lewis, Daniel, s. Chas. and E. M., *d.* Oct. 7, 1717,
LeCoulier, Anne, wf. Dudley, *b.* Jan. 12, 1762.
Livingston, Cæsar, *d.* Sept. 16, 1732.
Lucas, Henry E., Jr., *b.* Mch 2, 1869, age 40, Pompion Hill.
 Augustus, *b.* Dec. 2, 1870, age 30, Pompion Hill.

M

Martin, Richard, *d.* Oct. 21, 1713.
 Samuel, *b.* Sept. 23, 1801, age 13, Brick Church.
 John, *b.* Mch 18, 1829, age 36.
 Infant of S. T., *b.* Ap'l 5, 1857, Brick Church.
 Samuel T., *b.* Feb. 4, 1859, age 36, Brick Church.
 William Henry, *b.* Ap'l 1863, age 18, Brick Church.
Maxwell, Peter James, s. Jas. and Mary, *d.* May 29, 1732.
Matthews, John, *b.* Nov. 21, 1749.
Mayer, ——, wf. Dr. Lawrence, *b.* Aug. 12, 1769.
 Dr. Lawrence, *b.* Nov. 22, 1777, Plantation.
Marion, Hester, wf. Benj. *b.* Mch 1, 1760.
 James, s. James, *b.* Feb. 13, 1764, Plantation.
 Mary, wf. John, *d.* Jan. 15, 1765, Brick Church.
 Paul, s. James and Mary, *d.* May 2, 1765, Plantation.
 Sarah, wf. John, *b.* Jan. 17, 1765, Brick Church.
 James, *b.* Jan. 15, 1769, Plantation.
McGrigory, Martha, *b.* Ap'l 22, 1750.
McDowell, Geo. Arch'ld., *b.* Sept. 13, 1839, age 2, Brick Ch.
 Susan Taylor, Mrs., *b.* July 22, 1844, age 25,
 Brick Church.
 George, *b.* Feb. 14, 1864, age 20, Brick Church.
 Wm. B., *b.* Nov. 25, 1870, age 66, Brick Church.
Miller, ——, *d.* May 1, 1732.
 ——, wf. Stephen, *b.* Jan. 7, 1740, age 48.

Miller, John, b. Dec. 30, 1740, age 63, Brick Church.
  Sarah, d. Stephen, b. Oct. 22, 1755.
  Martha, wf. Stephen, b. May 20, 1763, Brick Church.
  Martha, wf. Stephen, Jr., b. June 16, 1763, age 34,
    Brick Church.
  Elizabeth, b. Aug. 30, 1762, Plantation.
  Elizabeth, b. Aug. 10, 1764, age 20 mos., Brick Ch.
  Martha, b. May 26, 1773, age 53, Brick Church.
  Stephen, Col., b. May 27, 1776, Brick Church.
Miles, Moses, b. Dec. 31, 1770, Pompion Hill.
Monk, Thomas, b. Mch 4, 1713.
Mouzon, ——, d. Lewis, d. May 16, 1745.
Moore, John, Esq., d. June 24, 1788, age 62, Brick Church.
  Elizabeth, wf. John, Esq., d. Dec. 15, 1790, age 53,
    Brick Church.
  John Elias, Esq., d. Nov. 29, 1811, age 49, Brick Ch.
Morrain, Paul, b. May 24, 1745.
Muirhead, Dr. Robert I., b. Sept. 28, 1872, age 33, Hob-Craw,
    Christ Church.
Myers, John, b. Oct. 5, 1849, age 42, Charleston.

N

Nelson, Edward, inf. s. Capt., b. May 6, 1874, Methodist Ch.
  Oscar, b. Oct. 5, 1874, age 4, Methodist Church.

O

O'Hear, Abbie, d. Dr. John, b. July 12, 1861, Brick Church.
Orum, Sarah, d. Joseph and Frances, d. Sept. 22, 1764, Plan-
    tation.

P.

Pagett, Ann, wf. Francis, b. Feb. 28, 1732–3.
  John s. John, Esq., b. Oct. 13, 1744.
  ——, wf. Francis, b. July 26, 1746.
  John, Esq., b. Nov. 29, 1747.
Palmer, Wm. Manly, b. Nov. 26, 1856, Brick Church.

Parker, John, *d.* Feb. 3, 1804, age 45, Brick Church.

        Elizabeth, Mrs. R., *d.* Dec. 13, 1809, age 43, Br. Ch.

        George, *d.* Aug. 22, 1811, age 52, Brick Church.

        Benjamin, *d.* April 9, 1825, age 59, Brick Church.

        Martha, Mrs., *d.* Nov. 22, 1826, age 58, Brick Church.

        Samuel, *d.* May 8, 1830, age 62, Brick Church.

        Elizabeth M., *d.* Sep. 26, 1830, age 27, Brick Church.

        John V., *d.* July 7 1837, age 41, Brick Church.

        Maria L. Mrs., *d.* Aug. 7, 1843, age 38, Brick Church.

        Sarah Elizabeth, *d.* Aug. 7, 1843, Brick Church.

        Robert Lawrence, *d.* Nov. 9, 1847, age 32, Brick Ch.

        William Roper, *d.* July 24, 1851, age 27, Brick Ch.

        Martha D., *d.* Oct. 16, 1851, age 23, Brick Church.

        Peter G., *d.* June 22, 1852, age 53, Brick Church.

        Samuel Daniel, *d.* Nov. 27, 1858, age 46, Brick Ch.

Peredon, Sarah, *b.* Dec. 2, 1767.

Pemberton, Dr. William, *d.* Sep. 18, 1732.

Pinckney, Roger, Esq., *b.* Mch. 2, 1776.

Poitvine, Peter, s. Peter and Susannah, *d.* Dec. 1, 1722.

Pollock, John, Rev., *b.* Oct. 26, 1712.

        Joseph John, s. Rev., *b.* Dec. 26, 1713.

Poyas, John Lewis, *b.* June 19, 1845, age 35, Daniel's Island.

        James D., s. Samuel, *b.* Jan. 5, 1867.

        C. Elizabeth, wf. Samuel H., *b.* July 5, 1877, Meth. Ch.

Q

Quash, Robert, *b.* April 3, 1772, Pompion Hill.

        Susannah, wf. Robert, *d.* July 24, 1774, Pomp. Hill.

        Constantia, wf. Robert, *d.* Feb. 21, 1775, Pomp. Hill.

        Elizabeth W., *b.* Sep 20. 1790, Pompion Hill.

        Sarah W., d. R. and C., *b.* Aug. 31, 1821, Pomp. Hill.

        Robert Hasell, *b.* Nov. 9, 1846, Pompion Hill.

        Francis Dallas, *b.* ——, 1857, Pompion Hill.

R

Reid, James, *b.* Nov. 25, 1748.

Rembert, C. D., Mrs. *b.* Nov. 8, 1872, age 73, Brick Church.

        Amanda, Mrs. *b.* ——, 1875.

Reab, { George, Charlotte, } twins, *b.* Mch. —, 1851, Pompion Hill.

Rogerman, John, *b.* Feb. 17, 1713-14.

Rowes, James, s. James, *d.* Sep. 30, 1727.

Roche, Rebecca, wf. Francis, *b.* Dec. 19, 1744.

    Anne, d. Francis and Anne, *b.* Dec. 30, 1770.

    Francis, —— ——

Roach, Ann, wf. Francis, *b.* Oct. 12, 1763, Pompion Hill.

Rollain, James, Sr., *b,* ——, 1754.

    ——, widow, James, Sr., *b.* Oct. 31, 1755.

Roulain, Abraham, *b.* April 26, 1760.

    James, s. James, *b.* Feb. 22, 1771.

    James Oliver, s. James, *b.* Aug. 6, 1773.

    ——, wf. James, *b.* Oct. 24, 1773.

Ronan, Geo. Washington, *d.* May 6, 1846, age 35, Brick Ch.

Robertson, William, *b.* July 30, 1870, age 76, Brick Church.

Russ, John, Sr., *d.* July 1, 1717.

    Jonathan, Sr., *d.* Feb. 27, 1726-7.

    Eliza, d. Jonathan, *d.* May 18, 1731.

    Mary Ann, d. Jonathan, *d.* May 19, 1731.

    Martha, d. Jonathan, *d.* May 25, 1731.

    Eliza, d. David and Elizabeth, *d.* Oct. 7, 1731.

    ——, s. David and Elizabeth, *d.* April 15, 1733.

    Jonathan, s. Jonathan, *b.* April 18, 1758.

    Jonathan, Sr., *b.* Feb. 18, 1763, Kainhoy.

Russell, Jeremiah, *b.* Feb. 25, 1748.

    Mary, *b.* Aug. 1, 1763, Plantation.

    Elizabeth, *d.* Aug. 11, 1762, Plantation.

S

Sallens, Thomas, s. Peter and Freelove, *d.* June 16, 1722.

Sanders, Sarah, widow, *d.* Jan. 6, 1750-1.

    John, *d,* June 17, 1743.

    John, *b.* Jan. 22, 1758, Brick Church.

    Mary, widow, *b.* April 4, 1760, Cainhoy.

    William, *b.* June —, 1763 Charleston.

    Thomas, s. John, Sr., *b.* Oct. 12, 1763, Brick Ch.

    Mary Ann, wf. Thomas, *b.* Sep. 4, 1765, Brick Ch.

Sanders, Joseph, b. Nov. 20, 1777, Brick Church.

John, d. Jan. 7, 1846, age 19, Brick Church.

Matilda, d. Wm. and Mary, b. Mch. 30, 1857, age 1, Brick Church.

William, b. April 12, 1858, age 36, Brick Church.

Thomas, b. Dec. 16, 1862, age 36, Brick Church.

George R., b. Oct. 13, 1867, age 30, Brick Church.

Elizabeth Francis, d. Samuel and Emma, b. Jan.22, 1868, Brick Church.

Savineau, Elizabeth, b. Dec. 17, 1769.

Serre, Noah, b. Nov. 10, 1752, Brick Church.

Shute, John, b. Mch. 30, 1760, Brick Church.

Simons, Anthony, s. Peter, d. Sep. 19, 1722.

Francis, d. June 8, 1731.

Catharine, d. Oct. —, 1731.

Mary Esther, d. April 14, 1737.

—— widow Peter, Esq., d. Dec. 20, 1745.

Peter, b. June 26, 1748.

Francis, s. ——, b. April 13, 1749.

——, d. Samuel, b. Nov. 5, 1750.

Anne, wf. Benjamin, b. April 21, 1754.

Samuel, s. Benjamin, b. Nov. 4, 1756.

Elizabeth, wf. Francis, b. Dec. 1766, Plantation.

Francis, s. Francis and Elizabeth, b. Feb. 13, 1767.

Benjamin, s. Benjamin, Jr., b. Aug. 3, 1771.

Francis, b. Oct. 4, 1771, Pompion Hill.

Benjamin, Esq., b. May 1, 1772, Pompion Hill.

Edward, s. Benjamin, b. June 25, 1773.

Lydia, d. Benjamin, b. Sep. 27, 1774.

Benjamin, Jr., at Scott's Ferry, b. April 26, 1776.

Benjamin, b. Dec. 7, 1780, Pompion Hill.

Catharine W., b. Nov. 8, 1820, Pompion Hill.

Simmons, Maurice, d. April 8, 1845, age 59, Brick Church.

Rachel, b. April 24, 1851, Brick Church.

Singletary, ——, wf. Jonathan, d. Feb. 25, 1732.

Jonathan, b. June 17, 1750.

Elizabeth, b. —— ——

Elizabeth, wf. Thomas, b. Oct. 5, 1772.

Singletary, Thomasin, d. John, *b.* Dec. 8, 1773.

Sloan, Allen, *b.* April —, 1876, Methodist Church.

Smith, Dr. Thomas Stitt, *b.* April 1, 1734.

Snow, Mary, d. James and Esther, *d.* Mch. 18, 1723–4.

    Esther, *d.* Mch. 28, 1723–4.

    Sarah, widow, *b.* Jan. 21, 1765, Brick Church.

Songster, Andrew, *d.* May 9, 1725,

Strand, Elizabeth, *b.* Feb. 27, 1731–2.

Strahan, John, *b.* Oct. 31, 1743.

Stone, John, s. Joseph, *b.* June 4, 1750.

    ——, wf. Joseph, *b.* Oct. 25, 1753.

St. Martin, Sarah. wf. John, *d.* Oct. 30, 1725.

    ——, infant child of Mr., *b.* May 5, 1857, Br. Ch.

Steele, John S., *b.* Feb. 22, 1829, age 30.

    Sarah A., Mrs., *b.* Oct. 23, 1845, age 48, Brick Church.

Staneer, Moses, s. N. (B. B. S.) *b.* June 19, 1862, age 7, Br. Ch.

Stifvater. Juliana, *b.* Dec. 30, 1853, age 10, Cox's Place.

Sweetman, Robert, *d.* Sep. 14, 1726.

Syer, Anna, wf. Robert, *b.* May 15, 1709.

    Robert, *b.* Aug. 21, 1710.

Syme, Elizabeth, *b.* Sep. 21, 1757, Brick Church.

    Andrew, *b.* Dec. 16, 1773, Brick Church.

T

Tart, John, *b.* Oct. 27, 1745, Brick Church.

    Sarah, wf. Nathan, *b.* Nov. 21, 1757.

    Priscilla, wf. Nathan, *d.* Aug. 22, 1766.

    Nathan, *b.* Feb. 27, 1768, Cainhoy Meeting.

    Elizabeth, d. Nathan, *b.* June 18, 1777.

Tavel, Charles, *b.* Nov. 21, 1836, age 43.

Taylor, ——, *b.* Aug 25, 1751.

Thomas, Elizabeth. wf. Samuel, *b.* Mch 24, 1755.

    Elizabeth Ashby, d. Samuel, *b.* Aug. 4, 1755.

    Two children of John, *b.* Nov. 13, 1768, Brick Ch.

    A child of Edward, *b.* May 9, 1778.

Tissott, John James, Rev., *b.* May 28, 1763, Pagett's old
    Plantation.

Tiencken, L. Anna, wf. John, *b*. Aug. —, 1876, age 19, Old Ruins.

Samuel Hamlin, *b*. Sept. —, 1876, Old Ruins.

Tousigere, Susannah, *b*. Mch 10, 1755.

John s. Stephen, B. B. S., *b*. Oct. 25, 1760, Brick Ch.

Tresivant, Theodore, *d*. Jan. 23, 1732.

——, Mrs., *d*. May 3, 1732.

Trouchet, Francis, *b*. Sept. 18, 1754.

Tyrrel, Walter, *d*. Nov. 22, 1840, age 65, Brick Church.

Edmund H.. *b*. Mch 3, 1872, age 56, Brick Church.

V

Varner, ——, *d*. July 27, 1733.

Vanderhorst, Elizabeth, wf. Arnoldus, *b*. Oct 19, 1761, Wappetaw, Christ Church.

Verone, ——, wf. Jeremiah, *d*. July 26, 1733.

Florence, *b*. Mch 20, 1862.

Venning, Brainard, *b*. June 22, 1868, age 40, Brick Church.

——, wf. Wm. C., *b*. Ap'l 10, 1869, Brick Church.

Oswald Freeman, Aug. 10, 1870, Brick Church.

Samuel Claudius, s. Wm. C., *b*. —, 1875, Brick Ch.

Pinckney Shingler, s. Wm. Lucas, *b*. Sept. —. 1876, age 6, Brick Church.

Ida Bee, infant, *b*. June 18 1882, Brick Church.

Videau, ——, wid. Henry, *b*. Oct. 9, 1772.

Henry, *b*. Ap'l 19, 1773, Pompion Hill.

W

Wallbank, John, s. John and Anna, *b*. Sept. 20, 1711.

Warnock, Martha, d. Andrew and Mary, *d*. June 19, 1713.

John, s. Andrew and Mary, *d*. Mch 6, 1716.

Samuel, *b*. Dec. 1, 1755.

——, wf. Abram, *b*. Jan. 31, 1770.

Walker, ——, wf. of Capt. Thos., *b*. Oct. 18, 1761, Plantation, Daniel's Island.

Capt. Thomas, *b*. Feb. 21, 1762, Plantation, Daniel's Island.

Watts, David, b. Jan. 7, 1777, Brick Church.

    Hester, d. Thomas, b. Nov. 1, 1770.

Wells, ——, wf. Samuel, b, Oct. 12, 1763, Cainhoy Meeting.

Westendorf, Adam M., d. Sept. 19, 1862, age 2, Brick Ch.

White, John, b. Feb. 22, 1749.

    ——, wf. John, b. June 7, 1774.

Witten, Margaret, d. Thos. and Elizabeth, d. Mch 31, 1728.

Williams, Elizabeth, wf. Daniel, b. Sept. 6, 1764, Padgett's.

    Daniel, d. Sept. 10, 1765, his plantation.

    ——, d. Daniel, d. Nov. 2, 1765.

Wilson, ——, wf. William, b. Sept. 3, 1770.

    ——, d. William, b. Sept. 10, 1770.

Wigfall, William, b. June 20, 1749.

    John, s. Thomas and Harriet, d. July 29, 1792, age 7 days, Brick Church.

    Thomas, s. Thomas and Harriet, d. Mch. 20, 1796, age 2 months, Brick Church.

    Eliza Moore, d. Thomas and Harriet, d. Oct. 9, 1797, age 2, Brick Church.

    Harriet, d. May 14, 1805, age 1, Brick Church.

    Harriet, Mrs., d. Dec. 2, 1807, age 35, Brick Church.

    Samuel, d. Oct. 15, 1830, age 29, Brick Church.

    Thomas, Jr., d. Feb. 9, 1840, age 41, Brick Church.

    William Moore, d. Nov. 3, 1841, age 39, Brick Ch.

    Thomas, Esq., d. Aug. 22, 1843, age 75, Brick Ch.

    John A., d. Mch. 5, 1845, age 54, Brick Church.

Wright, Thomas, s. William and Sarah, d, Dec. 22, 1721.

"Blessed are the dead who die in the Lord."—Rev. xiv.: 13.